inside..

Death Valley

FIFTH EDITION

by

Chuck Gebhardt

and

Tom Willis

A personal note to the reader:

Although the text of this book has been carefully evaluated, reviewed, and edited, discrepancies can sometimes occur. Your constructive criticisms, comments, or corrections are welcome for the benefit of future editions. Address your communications to the authors at:

CWG Creations
P. O. Box 5052
Pleasanton, Ca 94566
or
71213.3721@COMPUSERV.COM

Books by the author:
INSIDE DEATH VALLEY
BACKPACKING DEATH VALLEY

International Standard Book Number: 0-9601410-4-9
Library of Congress Card Catalog Number: 95-92423
Copyright © 1995 Tom Willis

In Memory

This book is dedicated to the memory of Chuck Gebhardt, my best friend and the creator of the original Inside Death Valley.

Chuck had a long term love affair with Death Valley. His long time hope and last wish was to have his memory kept with us, through the continued publication of his books.

A large part of my deep love for this desert is due to the wonderful memories of the more than 20 years Chuck and I spent walking and driving over virtually every inch of Death Valley. I'm positive his spirit is somewhere in the Valley, it is the closest thing to heaven we ever found.

It is mine and Chuck's sincere hope that you enjoy the park as much as we have over the years. Be sure to say "Hi", if we cross paths in the park.

Tom Willis

This book was written as a guide and reference text for Death Valley National Park. Its purpose is to educate and entertain. It is not intended as a survival guide nor is it to be interpreted as the final word regarding areas open to vehicles and/or visitors.

Since backcountry lands are subject to application of the Wilderness Act and either temporary or permanent closures for various reasons; it is the visitor's responsibility to verify such status before venturing into environmentally sensitive areas.

The author and CWG Creations have neither liability nor responsibility to any person or entity with respect to any loss or damage caused, or alleged to be caused, directly or indirectly, by the information contained in this book.

Acknowledgments

This book would not have been possible without all the help and support I was so fortunate to receive. Without a doubt Lupe Finch gave me the time, commitment, and the most support in getting the manuscript ready. This included proof reading, evaluation of content, and the countless uninterrupted hours with all my attention focused on a computer screen. I owe a great debt to Robert Spoecker for his time, company, and research assistance in the park. Patricia Smith gets a very special thank you for her knowledge and work in editing and proofing the final text. This book would not be as complete as it is without the support and assistance of Esy Fields of the Death Valley Natural History Association, and Glenn Gossard and Doug Threloff of the National Park Service.

Photo Credits

Anson Beman
    87

Chuck Gebhardt
    3, 6, 8, 17, 19, 21, 27, 29, 31, 35, 37, 39, 42, 43, 45, 47,
    49, 51, 57, 58, 61, 63, 65, 68, 71, 72, 74, 76, 77, 79, 81,
    83, 85, 89, 91, 93, 98, 100, 102, 109, 113, 119, 126, 127,
    128, 130, 135, 136, 137, 140, 141, 144, 148, 149, 150,
    155, 157, 158, 163, 165, 167, 168, 170, 172, 174, 178,
    179, 180,

Maxine Gebhardt
    117

National Park Service
    55, 134, 153,

Robert Spoecker
    123

Tom Willis
    1, 24, 32, 52, 106, 107, 111, 115, 121, 132, 133, 160,
    161,

U. S. Borax and Chemical Corp
    5, 10, 13, 15, 146

Table of Contents

4. Backcountry

5. Well, Here We Are

6. North Park

7. Center Park

8. South Park

Appendix A

Services Outside the Park

Appendix B

Distances

Bibliography

Index

Chapter 1
Historical View

Forming The Valley

Earth movement has shaped our world since prehistoric times. Death Valley was formed by earthquake activity rather than by glacial ice movement like Yosemite. Evidence of earthquake activity and power is apparent in the geologic structures and formations in and around the valley.

The depression that forms Death Valley is estimated to be between two and five million years old. Theories regarding the geology of the area indicate that the valley was formed by forces that pushed both the eastern and western mountains, which outline the valley, upward and apart. The resulting fault depression that remained has been filled in with material eroded from these mountains to form the valley floor. Some estimates are that the valley may be as deep as 8,000 feet, below the salt pan of Badwater and Devil's Golf Course.

Fault Scarp South Of Furnace Creek Inn

California is "earthquake country," and recent seismic activity has made for great headlines around the world. In the late 20th century Earthquakes near San Francisco and Los Angeles have changed the lives of thousands, if not millions, of people. Some excellent examples of seismic forces can be found throughout the state. But nothing provides a more dramatic picture of the results of earthquake activity than Death Valley. A very dramatic display of the effect of earth movement is within Titus Canyon, and is appropriately named "When Rocks Bend."

The last dramatic earthquake to occur in Death Valley happened about 2000 years ago. Some of the results from that quake can be viewed today, a short distance south of Furnace Creek Inn on the east side of Badwater Road. In places, you can see an escarpment about five feet high at the foot of the Black Mountains. This drop off is an indication of the powerful forces at work in forming the valley; the east side of the valley floor actually dropped about five feet in this earthquake. When you consider the damage wrought by the 1994 Northridge quake, near Los Angeles, that resulted in an eight inch shift; five feet is beyond comprehension.

One theory has it that at the time of this earthquake, 2000 years ago, the portion of the valley that is now a salt flat was actually the bottom of a small lake, about 30 feet deep. This lake is assumed to be the second time the valley floor was under water. The first lake, Lake Manly, filled the valley to a depth of about 600 feet during the Pleistocene Period. Evidence of these former lakes can be seen at many locations around the valley; at Shoreline Butte, Zabriskie Point, and on the way to Keane Wonder Mill.

Since the last major earthquake, the valley between the two mountain ranges has suffered few geological disturbances. Instead, the weather has worked upon the valley with oppressive heat and extreme dryness. Only the most tenacious of plants, animals, and people could hope to survive in this stringent environment. Today, the valley floor is the lowest point in the western hemisphere, 282 feet below sea level at two points near Badwater. The salt flat that can be seen around Badwater is the result of the drying of the lakes and the continued evaporation of ground water.

There is evidence of volcanic activity in Death Valley about 6 miles west of Scotty's Castle is Ubehebe Crater. This crater is the result of a massive explosion about 1000 years ago. Very near the southern rim of

this large crater is a series of smaller craters, the largest of these is Little Hebe crater. Little Hebe is actually a small cone shaped crater within a larger crater; immediately to the west of Little Hebe are two more small craters. All of these craters were formed by volcanic explosions rather than lava flows.

More evidence of volcanic activity is also present on the playa at the northern end of Panamint Valley, just to the north of Highway 190. This area has a heavy scattering of lava stones that appear to have been deposited by another volcanic explosion. The source of these volcanic stones is not readily apparent, nor is it addressed in any of the reference or research documents I have found. There is also a similar scattering, but not as concentrated, of volcanic stones near the Eureka Dunes in the Eureka Valley.

The First People

Anthropologists and archaeologists agree that the first Indians to come to North America migrated across the Bering land-bridge from Asia. From this point on, the nomadic habits of the tribes make it difficult for the scholars to reach further agreement as to their origin and the particular areas occupied by those tribes. Some of these prehistoric tribes were present in North America prior to the Ice Age, but much of the evidence of their existence was crushed and ground away by the recession of the ice sheets and glaciers.

This was not the case in Death Valley. The recession of the ice left behind a great lake, that later divided into two smaller ones -- Lake Manly in the south (Death Valley), and Lake Rogers in the north (Eureka Valley). Researchers have uncovered some evidence of the existence of primitive people here. Again, there are disagreements and many questions; where did these people come from, and what tribe had they originated from? Some say that the first Indians came from the north, Owens Valley, or the Mono Basin people. Others contend that all of the Death Valley native people originated from the Paiute or Shoshone.

Early studies by archaeologists and anthropologists give rise to three names for the groups of peoples known to have populated the Valley. The first group, called the Lake Mojave People, appeared around 8,000 BC. From the tool and weapon remnants discovered, the Lake Mojave People are considered to have been hunters. Sites disclosing the presence of the second group, the Mesquite Flat People, around 3,000 BC have been found. The Mesquite Flat People chose the cooler upper half of the Valley for their home. Since, by this time, the lake was gone and its former bed covered by a crust of salt. It is possible that Grapevine and Triangle Spring off Mesquite Flat, and McLean Spring to the south were sources of water for these people. Just prior to the phenomena that created a lake for the second time in the southern part of the Valley, a third group called Saratoga Spa people appeared. This last group was forced to adapt to a more harsh environment than their predecessors. They eked out a living on the sparse vegetation and minimal game available.

In the days of the forty-niners the Indians populating the area were mostly small family units rather than tribal communities which we tend to associate with the Native American culture. These families were located at the water sources throughout the valley.

When white men first came to the valley, their understanding was that the Indians called themselves the Panamint people. Some texts and displays still make references to the Panamint Indians. Research has shown that even the early Indians were related to the Shoshone people.

The Shoshone people were found in the Valley at the mouth of Furnace Creek, near Bennett's Well, and at Grapevine Springs. The Paiute people were found to the east at Ash Meadows, and to the southeast near Tecopa. Today, the descendants of the early Death Valley Indians are known as the Timbisha Shoshone.

There are many folk stories about the role of the Indians in the Valley during the days of the forty-niners and the prospectors that came later. Some of the key figures are Panamint Tom, his brother Hungry Bill, Indian George, and Shoshone Johnny. Hungry Bill was an army scout, and later a farmer who reportedly sold food to some of the prospectors in the area. He maintained a small ranch near the top of Johnson Canyon.

Panamint Tom was the chief of the Shoshone in the latter part of the 1800s. He made a name for himself by stealing horses from ranches as far south as Los Angeles. These horses were used primarily as food, and Panamint Tom would return from his forays, to drop off horses to each of his scattered bands, the number depending on how many people they had to feed. However, the horse stealing idea was not completely his own; perhaps he learned of this lucrative food source from Paiute braves, or from the raiding parties, made up of white men, who would steal horses

Old Dinah

from the herds being driven east by traders. In any case the horse-meat diet was a luxury for the Indians. Panamint Tom is known to have a second less colorful reputation; he would routinely rescue lost prospectors from certain death in the desert.

The normal diet of the desert Indians consisted mainly of the sparse plant and animal life in the Valley. The three most common foods were derived from the Pinyon Pine, Beavertail Cactus, and Mesquite.

In September when the Indians were preparing to return to the warmer valley for the winter, they would gather Pinyon Pine Nuts. On the upper slopes of the Panamints, all available women would attack the pines with long forked sticks to beat or pull down the cones. Using large conical baskets, they would collect the fallen cones and carry them back to the base camp. A large fire would be built in a mound of rocks on which the cones were placed to smolder and force the scales open. The dried cones would then be beaten with rocks, and the loosened nuts shaken or brushed out of the cones. Special baskets were used to screen out the nuts and separate them from the scales and bits of cones. It has been said that a dozen women could gather two bushels, about 44 pounds, of nuts in one day. The nuts were shaken in a basket of live coals until roasted.

Coyote Melon

When the roasting is complete and the shells are removed, the nuts may be eaten as is or ground in a wooden mortar to be used for soup.

Almost anything was fair game among the desert animals the Indians used as food: Pack Rats, Kangaroo Rats, Squirrels, Rabbits, Lizards, Coyote, and Bighorn Sheep. The majority of these animals were caught either by use of dead-fall traps or by being driven into woven grass nets by bands of Indians. Although a reporter, John Spears of the *New York Sun*, visiting the Valley in 1892, wrote:

> "While at the ranch (Furnace Creek Ranch), it was visited by a native sportsman - a little black, dirty Paiute. He was dressed in cast-off clothing of white men, and was armed with a bow and three arrows. The bow was of Juniper backed with raw sinew, and the arrows were of reed tipped with Juniper. They were effective against rabbits, rats, and lizards, and so satisfactory to the Paiute sportsman. The Indians had burned some acres of Mesquite and brush along Furnace Creek in their hunting for rabbits and rats. There is very little meat about them, but everything is fish that comes to the Paiute net, including Kangaroo Rats."

The Bighorn Sheep were infrequent game for the Valley Indians. One source states that they were hunted with bow and poison arrows; the poison was made from dried sheep's blood. Hunting the sheep was carefully planned and executed. The best Indian marksmen were established in stone blinds along trails leading to the many springs. The remaining Indians of the hunting party would act primarily as "brush-beaters" and attempt to drive the unaware sheep past the blinds.

Despite their difficulties in obtaining the limited food available and the forced migration to the mountains in the summer and return in winter, the Shoshone were relatively satisfied with their lot in Death Valley. That is, until the coming of the white man and the changes they brought while attempting to capture the mineral wealth of the desert.

Today, distant descendants of the early people remain in the Valley. There are presently about 40 families of the Timbisha Shoshone Tribe residing in the Indian Village south of Furnace Creek Ranch. These people are permanent residents of the area. There are no other Native American tribes in the Valley.

Covered Wagon

Wagon Train To California

It was on Christmas Day in 1849 that the first white men gazed down into Death Valley. They had come over miles of desert and mountains seeking a shortcut to California. Below this pioneer's gaze lay the end of Furnace Creek Wash and two small bands of Shoshone Indians. The Indians offered the only greeting they knew; during the first night of the white men's encampment, three of their oxen were wounded by Shoshone arrows.

This pioneer group was a small remnant of a large party of gold seekers called the Sand Walking Company, a name distorted from their destination, the San Joaquin Valley. During the early fall of 1849, the original party of about 107 wagons congregated at Salt Lake to decide upon the best route to California. The Sand Walking Company, led by Captain Jefferson Hunt of the Mormon Battalion, was overtaken by another wagon train led by Captain Smith. This new train had in its possession a map indicating an easier route through the southern mountains whereby the pioneers could escape the fate of the Donner Party. Hunt's train then broke up into what is now called the Death Valley Party, which consisted of the Bennett, Arcane, Wade, and Brier families, and a group of young men called the Jayhawkers.

About 26 wagons made it into Death Valley. The Jayhawkers split off, heading north, to find their own way out of the valley. They camped at in the area of McLean Spring, near present day Stovepipe Wells Village. The Jayhawkers eventually burned all of their wagons, slaughtered some of their oxen, smoked the meat, and found their way out through Townes Pass. The Bennett, Arcane, Brier, and Wade families moved south to what is now known as Bennett's Long Camp. The Wade family camped with the Bennett-Arcane group for a short while. They headed south by themselves and gradually worked their way out of the Valley, past Saratoga Springs, with their wagon. The Wade's were the only family to get a wagon out intact.

Biographical accounts, personal letters, and a scattering of diary notes attribute the sufferings of the Bennett-Arcane Party to the heat and a lack of food and water. However, they were camped near a spring, in the winter and had livestock available to slaughter for food. All things considered, it is apparent that these forty-niners suffered more from psychological shock than physical discomfort. They felt the emotional strain and frustration of being at some place different than intended, and the seemingly insurmountable difficulty facing them to find a way out of the valley.

The Bennett-Arcane party was guided by a young man named William Lewis Manly. He and another young man, John H. Rogers, decided to search for a route out of the Valley. Taking their guns and what few supplies that could be spared, they left for a planned two week journey. Some 26 days later they returned with some supplies, after having found what might pass for a route and civilization. The Bennett and Arcane group and the Briers were the only people in the camp. The others having left thinking that Manly and Rogers would not return once out of the desert. The entire party moved out of the Valley over the Panamint Mountains with their belongings and four children loaded on oxen.

On the second day of their journey out of the valley, they crossed the summit of the Panamint Range exclaiming "Good-bye, Death Valley." This is reportedly the origin of the name, although it is stated by three separate authors as having been spoken by Mrs. Brier, Mrs. Bennett, and Mr. Manly. Regardless of the honor to whom the naming belongs, it was somewhat suitable. Contrary to popular stories, only one of the original forty-niners died during this unplanned trip into the Valley.

White Gold

For almost 20 years following the departure of the forty-niners, Death Valley was relatively quiet. A handful of prospectors and other hopefuls explored the Valley in those years looking for gold or silver. Their efforts were mostly in vain. Some were looking for the "big find," and others were satisfied with the just the feel of freedom and lack of responsibility.

The most significant event which revealed Death Valley to the world was the discovery of borax. This little known mineral rapidly became so well known that even long-time prospectors gave up their search for lost gold and silver mines. Men become millionaires overnight, and still others became rich one year, broke the next, only to discover another pocket of borax and start the cycle again the year after that.

In the valley, the period from 1875 to 1914 by itself reflected the turmoil of the times. New companies were forming, and there were mergers with other borax organizations. We have mines being depleted simultaneous with new borax finds. At the same time financial titans were going bankrupt. All this leads to confusion as to how and when events took place.

I have arranged the Death Valley borax story in chronological order. I cannot guarantee its absolute accuracy as, in the case of most histories,

Gathering Borax At Cottonball Marsh

opinions vary. There are many discrepancies in the facts as depicted by different sources, but this is to be expected of accounts that were transcribed second, third, and even fourth hand. As best as I can determine, this is how the borax story is written:

1861   Prospecting south of the Inyo Range, John Searles discovered borate deposits at what is now Searles Lake. It wasn't until 1872 that Searles incorporated as the San Bernadino Borax Company and started production. This company was later sold to the Pacific Coast Borax Company.

      Although the ownership of the company has changed many times, the mud from this dry lake is still used for producing borates and potash today. This production is probably the single economic reason for the existence of the town of Trona, which started as a "company town" in support of the mining operations.

1871   William Troup found some cottonball (a borate mineral) at Columbus Marsh and Salt Wells in Nevada. These and other discoveries in Lake County, California considerably reduced the importation of borax, and decreased the cost to about $0.38 a pound.

1872   Francis Marion Smith, later to be known as the Borax King or Borax Smith, had been supplying wood to the Columbus Marsh operation. His cabin was close to Teel's Marsh (Nevada), where he had noticed deposits similar to those at Columbus Marsh. He took a sample to an assayer and the sample proved to be the richest specimen of cottonball yet found. Smith's strike was not secret very long, and he battled to keep claim jumpers from taking over his discovery. Eventually he won out and formed the firm of Smith and Storey Brothers. Soon afterward, the Chicago firm of Storey Brothers sold their interests to Smith and the new company became known as the Smith Brothers.

1875   Isadore Daunet, on a prospecting trip through Death Valley, picked up some samples of borate mineral from the west side of the salt flat. Although he paid no particular attention to their significance at the time, he did hold onto these samples for the next six years.

1881 Aaron Winters and his wife Rosie lived in abject poverty at Ash Meadows, Nevada. Winters was a desert prospector with a history for unlucky finds. A traveler stopping to share a meal with the Winters' showed them some samples of cottonball from the north. Aaron remembered seeing lots of that material all over the floor of Death Valley. The next morning, Aaron and Rosie went to the Valley and collected some cottonball north of Furnace Creek, tested it with sulfuric acid and alcohol, and Aaron exclaimed, "She burns green! Rosie, by God, we're rich!" Aaron sent samples to the W.T. Coleman Company of San Francisco for an assay. Several weeks later a Coleman representative handed Winters a check for $20,000.00.

1881 Daunet got word of the Winters' discovery and remembered the deposits he had found. He assembled a few partners and fifty men to gather borax and established the Eagle Borax Works. For almost two years Daunet struggled with borax production. The material he shipped was so impure he could get only $0.08 a pound. Three years and 130 tons of borax later, Daunet committed suicide and the entire operation was abandoned.

1882 A prospector for the W.T. Coleman Company discovered Colemanite, a form of borate, in the Funeral Mountains. During this year and the next, the borax fever was widespread. Many more important discoveries of Colemanite were made at Monte Blanco in Furnace Creek Wash, and the Calico Mountains. Coleman managed to purchase the Calico Mine.

1882 Coleman constructed the Harmony Borax Works near the marsh (Cottonball Marsh) of Winters' discovery. Cottonball gathering was accomplished by Chinese laborers.

1883 Borax was discovered in the Amargosa Desert. Coleman bought the property for $15,000.

1884 Since the Harmony Borax Works was too hot to work during the summer months, Coleman moved his operations to the Amargosa area where the high desert was cooler. He organized two new companies the Harmony Borax Mining Co. and the Meridian Borax Company.

1885   Borax Smith kept busy acquiring borax properties around Columbus Marsh. After dissolving the partnership with his brother Julian the year before, Smith hired Christian Zabriskie to be superintendent of his newly formed Pacific Borax Salt and Soda Company. Simultaneously, he organized the Teel's Marsh Borax Company as the successor firm to Smith Brothers. With these new formations, Smith became the largest producer of borax in the United States. Most all of his borax shipments were handled by the W.T. Coleman Company, and Coleman later served as sole agent.

1888   In the mid 1880s, Coleman started development work to process the Colemanite ore at his Calico mine.

In the spring of 1888, W.T. Coleman Company failed and went into bankruptcy. All of Coleman's property passed into the hands of assignees, and in 1890 the entire assets were deeded to Smith. Smith consolidated these holdings into the Pacific Coast Borax Company.

Borax Company Poster - Circa 1884

1893   Stephen Mather, later to be founder and first director of the National Park Service (1916), joined Pacific Coast Borax Company as a super salesman. It was Mather who was responsible for the use of the 20-Mule Team trademark.

1907   The Lila C. Mine (named for Coleman's daughter) started production when Calico became depleted.

1914   Smith, diversified and involved in numerous financial ventures suffered financial collapse and was forced to resign.

1925   This year saw the close of 43 dramatic years of borax production in the Death Valley region. The following year Furnace Creek Inn was built, putting the Pacific Coast Borax Company in the hotel business for 40 years.

1933   Death Valley National Monument established by presidential proclamation.

1959   The Harmony Borax Works property was deeded to the National Park Service by the U.S. Borax and Chemical Corporation.

1976   The "Mining In Parks Act" was passed by Congress. This closed Death Valley to new mining claims being filed, limited the scope of open-pit mining, and allowed the Park Service to begin managing all mining activity within the Park.

1991   Although approximately 140 active mining claims remain within the Park, only a few are being worked. The Billie Mine, an underground borate mine, is the most visible on the way to Dante's View. The Crater Claim Group, a sulfur mine at the top of Hanging Rock Canyon is just outside the park boundary.

The preceding chronological account of borax history is a small part of a much larger picture. Other famous names and places are involved within the framework of the dates listed, but contributed to borax history rather than made it. One important single factor in the early development and success of borax was the 20-Mule Team. Roads and rails were few and far between in the territories where borax was discovered. The ingenious

Borax Smith was responsible for the building of the Tonopah and Tidewater, Borate and Daggett, and Death Valley Railroads. Although these were tremendous feats in themselves, they were not as spectacular as the accomplishments of the 20-Mule Team.

20 Mule Team

The establishment of Harmony Borax Works and the acquisition of the Amargosa Works presented immediate transportation problems to W. T. Coleman. He purchased a 12-mule outfit that had hauled ore for the Eagle Borax Works. Ed Stiles, their driver, was more than just a competent "mule skinner." Before he was twenty, Ed had hauled freight all over the desert regions around Death Valley. He knew the water-holes, hidden canyons, and short cuts that connected important mining areas with railheads. To augment the 12-mule outfit, Coleman bought an 8-mule rig that had hauled for a Nevada freight line Coleman had once hired to move his borax before production became extensive.

It wasn't long before someone figured out that if both teams could be joined as one with larger wagons, many hauling problems could be solved.

20-Mule Team South Of Furnace Creek

Laid out as one team, the mules stretched ahead for over 100 feet in front of the driver. Ed Stiles handled them like an expert, and continued to do so for another two and a half years.

Jim Dayton was hired by Coleman's company as a swamper working with Ed Stiles for a short time. Jim then went on to manage Greenland Ranch, now Furnace Creek Ranch. The ranch land was used to raise grain for the mules and as a repair station for the wagons.

Although the outfits were called 20-Mule Teams, they were actually made up of 18 mules and 2 horses. To befit the size of the new team, wagons had to be designed to fit the potential load they could now handle. The U.S. Borax and Chemical Corporation explains the design:

> "When the blueprints were finished, they called for wagons with rear wheels 7 feet high and front wheels 5 feet high, each with steel tires 8 inches wide and 1 inch thick. The hubs were 18 inches in diameter and 22 inches in length. The spokes, of split oak, measured 5 ½ inches wide at the hub and 4 inches wide at the point. The axeltrees were made of solid steel bars, 3 ½ inches square. The wagon boxes were 16 feet long, 4 feet wide, and 6 feet deep. Each wagon, empty, weighed 7,800 pounds. A complete compliment consisted of two box wagons and a water wagon. Two loaded box wagons, plus the weight of the water tank, which carried 1,200 gallons, made a total load of 73,200 pounds or 36 ½ tons."

The wagons were built by Studebaker and cost about $900 each. They were in constant operation for five years and never had a breakdown. The original route from Harmony Borax Works was 165 miles long through the salt flats, over Wingate Pass, past Searles Lake, into Mojave, all in about 10 days. An entire round trip would take 30 days. On the return trip the wagons would bring water and feed to restock the way-stations along the route.

During the 1890's while the Borate and Daggett Railroad was under construction, the 20-Mule Teams were again pressed into service to haul for the Calico mine. In 1907, while the Death Valley Railroad spur to the Tonopah and Tidewater Railroad was built, the 20-Mule Teams were

used again. Still no breakdowns. In 1937, two 20-Mule Teams made it over the original route to Mojave without a single breakdown. Today, one set of wagons is on display in front of Furnace Creek Ranch. Another is on a terrace next to the ruins of Harmony Borax Works. A third set is at the visitor's pavilion next to the borate pit mine at Boron, California.

Prior to the construction of the railroad between the Calico mine and Daggett, Borax Smith began to consider the 20-Mule Team system outmoded. In 1894, he purchased a coal-burning traction engine called "Old Dinah" and two ore wagons for the 12 mile trip from the mine to Daggett. Other than the ton and a half of fuel that Old Dinah consumed each trip, and the slow speed of three and a half miles per hour, the tractor had a habit of digging in when traveling over soft sand. Going up steep grades was a challenge for Old Dinah, for even with a ton and a half of sand bags on the front end, it would rear up and all control of steering would be gone. In less than a year the "Iron Mule" was abandoned and the mules put back into service.

In 1909, Old Dinah was sold to Joseph Lane of Rhyolite. He started the Keane Wonder Traction Company and used the tractor to haul freight and supplies over Daylight Pass to Keane Wonder Mine. The new owners replaced the coal burning unit with an oil burner, but the "improvement" coupled with age caused Old Dinah to become explosive and the tractor was abandoned along side the Daylight Pass Road. In time, the borax company towed Old Dinah down to Furnace Creek Ranch where it stands near the remnants of the more successful 20-Mule Team wagons.

Although the California desert rang with the activities of borax prospectors and producers, the same era heard sounds of other prospecting ventures that add final touches of color to the history of Death Valley. The borax discoveries and their successful development contributed to whetting the appetites of desert adventurers. Surely there must be something else equal to the value of borax in the Valley to retain these wasteland wanderers. There were almost as many minerals to be discovered in the Valley as there were prospectors; tin, gold, manganese, copper, lead, silver, tungsten, and talc to name a few. The minerals and the people who searched for them have a history all their own.

Ghost Towns and Graves

The men, mines, and towns once populating the Death Valley region have since passed into history. They have left signs of their passing in various forms; rocks and crosses on graves, crumbling remains of towns, mines and mine tailings, and whole townsites reflecting their culture in the rubble of sardine cans, wire, and broken bottles. The late 1800s and early 1900s revealed the presence of mining on every one of the five major mountain areas of the Valley; Harrisburg, Panamint City, and Skidoo in the Panamints; Goldbelt in the Cottonwoods; Leadfield in the Grapevines; Chloride City and Keane Wonder in the Funerals; Furnace and Greenwater in the Black Mountains. Copper, gold, lead, and silver were the basic materials sought in these strange places, and some mines had sufficient quantities to make a few people rich, while others produced more excitement than money.

Shorty Harris was perhaps the undisputed champion prospector of Death Valley. Shorty's career lasted from the early 1880s to 1934 when he was put to rest next to his long time friend, Jim Dayton. Shorty has been reported to be the discoverer of the "big finds" of Bullfrog, Goldbelt, Harrisburg, St. Patricks, and World Beater. As rich as he was in friends and respect, he was poor in the pocketbook. Following one of his "finds," Shorty had the habit of extracting only enough ore to turn into cash for a year. He was a great story-teller, and would rather bend an ear than prospect. He was well liked by other prospectors; some would go to Shorty for advice on their claims and take every word he said as gospel truth. The Rhyolite/Bullfrog mine, discovered in 1904 and responsible for the booming of Rhyolite, could have made Shorty a millionaire. However, one story has it that he sold his interest to a bartender for about eight hundred dollars in order to buy "drinks all round."

The site of Skidoo rests on a rolling plateau at 5,700 feet in the Panamint Mountains. The surrounding area was so dry that water had to be piped from Telescope Peak, 23 miles away. Stories have it that the town's name was taken from a popular expression of the day, "23 Skidoo." One story is that an investor Bob Montgomery was buying up claims around Harrisburg. When his wife heard he was buying 23 claims she joked 23 Skidoo, hence the name of the mines and the town that grew around them. Another story links the name to the pipeline built to bring water to the town; it's up to you which you want to believe. The population of Skidoo peaked at about 700. It boasted of a post office, bank, stores, and the usual host of gold town saloons. After the financial panic of 1907 that had forced the decline of Rhyolite, Skidoo lost most of its financial backing and the $1.5 million it produced left town.

Stamp Mill At Skidoo

19

Today, passing the Park Service commemorative sign, staying on the right fork and climbing the slight rise beyond, you can visit a mill structure. The building housed a 15 stamp mill (actually three, 5-stamp batteries). This mill was used to crush the ore from the mines to aid in the removal the gold or silver.

Jean "Cap" Lemoigne was a mining engineer from Paris who signed-on for work at Eagle Borax Works only to find they were out of business upon his arrival. Lemoigne was an educated, serious, gentleman prospector. He worked around the Death Valley region for many years to gain enough capital to get his own claim. Reports indicate that a claim was discovered by Jean in 1918 in a canyon, that today bears his name, in the Cottonwood Mountains. Here Jean constructed a rock hut with a tin roof that stands to this day. A recent mining report states that the lead, silver, and zinc produced by this mine would have been worth $116,000 at January 1976 prices. Lemoigne worked only enough of his claim to meet his immediate needs, and in later years had a strong desire to return to his native Paris. Two different stories have emerged from the records concerning Jean's death. He left the safety of his canyon on a hot July day in 1925 to obtain supplies in Beatty; or he left because he was ill and went to Furnace Creek Ranch for help. Being in his eighties at the time and over 40 years as a prospector, the latter reason seems more likely. What is factual is that Jean "Cap" Lemoigne succumbed from the heat on the return trip to his mine from Furnace Creek Ranch. Some workers from the Ranch, being concerned about his safety, found his body north of the ranch and buried him.

Climbing out of the end of a canyon in the Funeral Mountains, like silent guardians, are the heavily timbered tramway towers of the fabulous Keane Wonder Mine. The now decaying mill, a mile below the mine, was reported to have 20 stamps processing 1800 tons of ore a month. This early 1900 gold boom was rumored to have made $750,000 before the vein ran out.

Directly above the Keane Wonder mine atop the cliffs of the Funeral Mountains was a city of silver - Chloride City. This city had two chances for a boom, but each time the ore simply did not have enough value to spark a real rush. Two efforts were made to profitably mine the area once in 1871 and again in 1909. In 1871 Eugene Lander, August Franklin, and a Mr. Hanson found what they thought was silver chloride. After they had pulled out about 100 tons of ore they were told it was actually lead chloride. Its value could not sustain the operation and the mine was closed in 1873. The mine was reopened by Irving Crowell in 1909; it was reported that he found some gold ore that assayed for about $35 a ton. Crowell lived at Chloride City until 1917, when he moved on to another mine near Beatty.

The import of Irish and Welsh miners brought the innovative "Cousin Jack" houses built into the hillsides. These houses were dug so that the rear and side walls (and sometimes the roof as well) were native dirt. All that had to be built was the front wall providing the door and perhaps a window. This permitted the miners to capitalize on their skill and minimize the expense of building materials. Some excellent examples of these houses still remain at the site of Chloride City and other locations around the valley.

The 1907 recession, depression, or financial panic (it has been referred to by all three titles in various publications) resulted in the death knell for another booming camp. Greenwater was going to be the "big bust" to end them all. The first several years of the 1900's saw hundreds of claims come and go - some good, some real losers. Those lucky enough to make their money in mining endeavors were anxious to double or triple their

Jean Lemoigne's Grave

fortunes by investing in promising claims. When copper was struck in the Black Mountains a mile above Death Valley, it didn't take long to find investors, sink shafts, and raise a town that would see 2,000 residents. The discoverers of the copper veins as well as the old timers in the region, who came on the run, had no doubts that Greenwater would far surpass Butte, Montana in copper output. In a very short time, the shafts were getting deeper and deeper, and so were the debts of the investors. It soon became obvious that the copper strike was minimal, as was the financial backing, and the town slowly strangled from lack of funds and mining activity.

Hidden from many visitors' view at the southern end of Death Valley where the paved highway turns to the east is the Ashford Mill ruins. A frustrating and exasperating series of misadventures were to plague the Ashford brothers, Harold, Henry, and Lewis, after their discovery of a ledge of gold in the Black Mountains. Although picking at ore from their mine in quantities adequate to feed them, the Ashfords had contracted to sell their mine for $100,000. The mine sale did not materialize due to the buyers default on the contract, and the Ashfords sued for possession and won. A little later, they took in a partner who foolishly decided to take a trip to see his mine and perished in the desert.

Another mineral, talc, was mined in Warm Springs Canyon, Galena Canyon and the Ibex Hills starting during World War II. The last operations were closed in 1988, and the property was purchased in 1989 by the Conservation Foundation. The land was donated to the Park Service in 1992 and as of this writing the mine sites are being made environmentally stable.

There is limited mining activity in the Death Valley area as of the end of 1994. Borate mining continues on a limited scale by the American Borate Company, near Ryan, in an underground mine. This mine, named the Billie Mine, can be observed from the road to Dante's View. However, the areas immediately around the mine and the site of Ryan are private property and closed to the public. The other significant active mining in the vicinity of Death Valley is the Bullfrog Mine near the site of Rhyolite, Nevada, the North American Chemical Co. borate and potash operation at Searles Lake in Trona, California, and the Crater Claim Group near Hanging Rock Canyon on Big Pine / Death Valley Road.

Chapter 2
Temperature and Topography

The Great Rectangle

Death Valley was established as a national monument in February 1933. It was changed to Death Valley National Park through Congressional action in October 1994. Within its boundaries is an area of approximately 5,189 square miles, or 3,321,000 acres, just about the size of the state of Connecticut, making it the largest national park in the lower 48 states.

The majority of the Park lies within California and encompasses Death Valley, Greenwater Valley, Saline Valley, the southern portion of Eureka Valley, and the northern end of Panamint Valley. A small northeastern section of the park, near Scotty's Castle, extends into Nevada (called the Nevada Triangle). Lastly a very small section of the park lies outside the park boundaries, northeast of Death Valley Junction. This is Devil's Hole a detached management unit within the Ash Meadows National Wildlife Refuge, Nevada.

There are six mountain ranges, of varying sizes, within the park. Starting on the eastern side of the park is the Greenwater Range which separates Greenwater Valley from the Amargosa Desert. The next mountains we encounter are the Amargosa Range; these mountains are the eastern border of Death Valley. On the west side of Death Valley is the Panamint Range, this range separates Death Valley from Panamint and Saline Valleys. Saline Valley is separated from the northern end of Panamint Valley by the Nelson Range. The Saline Range provides the separation between Saline and Eureka Valley. The Last Chance Range defines the eastern side of Eureka Valley. Lastly the northwestern boundary of the park lies at the foot of the Inyo Range. A map outlining the park and showing the approximate locations of the mountains and valleys is on the next page.

The Amargosa Range, on the east side of the Valley, is comprised of the Grapevine, Funeral, and Black Mountains. The Grapevine Mountains typically has the highest elevations, the two highest peaks are Wahguyhe Peak at 8,628 feet and, Grapevine Peak at 8,738 feet. The Funeral Mountains are host to Schwaub Peak at 6,448 feet and Pyramid Peak at

Death Valley
National Park

Relative Position Of Major
Mountains and Valleys
Not To Scale

© Tom Willis - 1995

6,703 feet. The Black Mountains are home to Dante's View at 5,475 feet, and Smith Mountain at 5,912 feet.

The northern portion of the Panamint Range is called the Cottonwood Mountains and is dominated by its highest peak, Tin Mountain at 8,953 feet. In the Panamint Mountains, to the south, is the highest mountain in the Park, Telescope Peak, with a commanding view at 11,049 feet. During the peak visitor season (Thanksgiving through Easter), Telescope Peak may be covered with snow, providing an unusual contrast with the arid scene at its feet. At the higher elevations the Panamint Range offers some large areas covered with Pinyon and Limber Pines, Desert Mahogany, and some Bristlecone Pines.

One of the best descriptive maps of the Valley is published by the Automobile Club of Southern California. It is entitled "Guide to Death Valley," map number 2578. Not only does it define the locations of most of the major points of interest, but it includes a brief written description of the more frequently visited sights.

A very informative topographic map, showing the new park's boundaries and a large number of key sites, is published by Tom Harrison Cartography and is available through map dealers. Reference maps to clarify directions and the locations of points of interest may be found throughout this book. However, they do not contain the amount of detail and information as the maps cited above.

Whenever I discuss Death Valley, I tend to divide it into separate and distinct entities. Speaking of Death Valley in general terms, I usually refer to it as the "Valley." This designation includes everything in my mind which is the topographical valley created by the mountainous barriers holding it captive on both the east and west. The second entity is the western portion of the park that was added in 1994; I usually refer to this entire area as Saline Valley.

Canyon Country

Of the 60 named canyons within the confines of the Park boundaries, well over fifty percent are accessible by vehicle. Some are limited to driving in for a distance and returning by the same route, while others are completely drive-through such as Titus Canyon, Echo Canyon and Grapevine Canyon. An equal number of canyons, washes, gorges, and gulches can be found outside of the Park boundary, some of which may be entered by vehicle, but many more are limited to foot traffic.

There are canyons whose names are personalized for some individual with a claim in the area or who met their demise while prospecting or exploring. Some of these are Ashford, Johnson, Lemoigne, Scotty's, and Titus Canyons. There are canyons whose names are self-explanatory providing the visitor with clues as to what to expect; Cork-screw, Dead Horse, Dry Bone, Grotto, Mosaic, Red Wall, and Talc Canyons. Such names as Chuckwalla, Golden, Mustard, and Sheep depict the natural and unnatural history of an area. One canyon name not difficult to explain is Titanothere Canyon, in the Grapevine Mountains. The word Titanothere describes an extinct rhinoceros-like animal from the Tertiary Period, 5 to 11 million years ago. At the Visitor's Center one can view the fossilized skull of a Titanothere found within this canyon.

This chapter will provide descriptions of canyons that are readily accessible to the majority of visitors. Chapter 4 will cover those canyons more difficult to traverse and requiring off-highway equipped vehicles.

Although Titus Canyon has become accepted as one of the most popular drive-through sights, it is not always passable by the average passenger car. However, you may easily traverse the two-way road up to the canyon mouth from the Death Valley side. A parking area is available near the mouth of the canyon from where you may hike into the canyon as far as you like to enjoy its breathtaking heights and narrowness. While walking the first mile into the canyon, be on the lookout for vehicles approaching you from around sharp bends. The narrowness of the canyon might make it a bit uncomfortable when a vehicle passes close, but keep in mind that you are not limited to the roadway as is the vehicle.

While in the vicinity of Stovepipe Wells Village, do not overlook a visit to Mosaic Canyon. The entrance road is on the south side of Highway 190 just at the west end of the Village. The 3 mile long, dusty road up the fan is sometimes rough and rutted, but passenger cars usually will not experience problems if driven slowly. A small parking area sits above the wash you will enter to start the hike. As in most of the Valley's canyons, the terrain is composed of gravel and sand and heading uphill. In a very short distance, you will round a bend and enter the first section of polished

Mosaic Canyon

walls. The wall on the left looks somewhat like polished marble, but take a moment to closely examine the wall immediately opposite this, on your right. What looks like a bunch of rocks embedded in mud is something altogether different; you'll find it is nature's way of making a mosaic. The next major bend in the canyon will bring you over a beautiful dry cascade normally covered with a layer of fine sand that will make the rock somewhat slippery. As you go deeper and deeper into the canyon, the walls get higher and higher exposing more of the polished mosaic which gave the canyon its name. Three-quarters of a mile through the first section, the canyon opens up into a larger canyon or wash. From here going to your right will take you to a series of minor canyons. These may be followed for at least another 5 miles with some strenuous climbing over dry waterfalls and fallen boulders.

Just off Furnace Creek Wash, about 5 miles east of the Furnace Creek Ranch along Highway 190, awaits 20-Mule Team Canyon. The one way road through this explorer's canyon is graded dirt, dusty, and about 3 miles in length. Drive in about 100 yards until you can see a "mine" opening in the hill to your right. Park out of the way, so as not to block traffic and walk up into the cleft to see, first-hand, the work of borax prospectors which is in evidence all through these multi-colored hills. The

27

first prospect on your right is approximately 20 to 30 feet deep and about 5 feet in height. Notice the reflections of light and color coming from the quartz and gypsum walls as the sun enters the small opening. Exercise extreme caution if you enter any of these diggings, probably the best advice is to look from outside the entrance. On up the hill to your left is a more extensive digging which might require the use of a strong light to get back any distance. All along the remaining portion of the drive, dozens of prospects can be seen dotting the sandstone hills about you. In the springtime, take time to stop alongside the road near the exit to view displays of wild flowers, like the Desert Five-Spot and the tiny, Desert Star plant.

Perhaps the second most popular canyon in the Valley is Golden Canyon, harboring a collection of brilliantly golden walls and sparkling side canyons. Golden Canyon is located 3 miles south of Furnace Creek Ranch on the east side of Badwater Road. A short road leads up to a parking area. This is an interpretative hike with trail guide pamphlets available at the canyon for $0.50. Start by hiking through the canyon to the end of the road, top the rise, and follow the right-hand wash to get to the base of spectacular Red Cathedral. It is best to view this massive wall of rock in the late afternoon to take advantage of the setting sun's accent on the coloring of the clefts. On the way out, take a trip up any or all of the minor canyons and washes passed along the way for unusual formations and rock hues. Along the south side will be a trail leading to Gower Gulch and up to Zabriskie Point. If you tire easy, this hike is simpler, if taken from Zabriskie Point and provides more views of the central Valley.

The Rains Came

The American Geological Institute defines a wash as "a Western Miner's term for any loose, surface deposits of sand, gravel, boulders, etc." Consulting the standard college dictionary produces a definition of "the dry bed of an intermittent stream." Getting right down into washes and canyons that have been named is perhaps the surest way of knowing one from the other. As an example, there are portions of 20-Mule Team Canyon that look like a wash, and places along Death Valley Wash that qualify as a canyon. My method for distinguishing between the two is simple and direct – if you're hiking along what appears to be an intermittent stream bed with sides that cannot be looked over without a ladder, you are in a canyon.

Alluvial fans are a by-product of the erosion that cuts the canyons. As the sand, gravel, and rock, technically called alluvium, is cut from the wash or canyon it is deposited at the mouth of the canyon, as the velocity of the water decreases. In the mountains, the rain and sometimes snow-melt contributes to the erosion of the material for building the fans. As long as the flow continues, there will always be some depositing of alluvium occurring.

Occasionally, stream flow may become so heavy and turbulent that the water takes new paths. In this case, the head of the fan may be eroded enough to cause cessation of a flow path down its normal route. An excellent example of this erosion and depositing of alluvium is visible on a fan along the road to Scotty's Castle, about 11.8 miles north of Highway 19. Watch for an interpretive sign on the east shoulder of the road.

A strange phenomenon that greatly disturbed me during my walks through Death Valley was what appeared to be large "dikes" across the width of the desert, formed by the alluvial fans. As an example, driving north from Furnace Creek Ranch and passing the Salt Creek turnoff, you will notice one of these "dikes" coming from the western side of the Valley out of Tucki Mountain and blocking any further view of what lies beyond.

These "dikes" are fans that have grown to monstrous proportions due to ideal conditions of mountain water runoff and material erosion. Driving south from Scotty's Castle, these huge fans consistently impede your line of sight to the approaching scenes of the lower valley. These "dikes" are doubly frustrating to the hiker moving down the Valley as progress is slow compared to driving. The relief at attaining the top of the rise created by a fan is soon crushed by the appearance of another off in the distance.

Sand Dunes

According to R.A. Bagnold, British military engineer, "The most typical kind of country on which desert dunes are found is a flat erosion surface, so arid that the complications introduced by rainfall and vegetation are negligible." Brigadier Bagnold has closely described the sand dune areas of Death Valley National Park. The most popular sand dunes in Death Valley start about one mile south of Triangle Spring and stretch south for 8 miles, coming to rest near Stovepipe Wells Village along Highway 190. The southern edge of the sand dune area parallels Highway 190 for about 5 miles east of Stovepipe Wells Village.

The major part of the Death Valley Sand Dunes area is at or below sea level and vegetation is not common in the general landscape. The formation of the large dunes in just that particular location is due to the availability of wind erodible material in the northern part of the valley. Bill Clark, a Park Naturalist, provided me with a theory on the formation of the sand dunes which is probably accurate. The winds driving down from the north of Mesquite Flat pick up particles of sand. Crossing the present sand dune area, the front of the sand-laden winds strike against Tucki Mountain and are forced upward and back on themselves creating a barrier of turbulence. As the barrier is approached by more sand-laden winds, their speed slows; since the velocity of the wind is the determining factor for holding the sand grains airborne, the sand falls to the valley floor. Mr. Clark also pointed out that the changing wind direction in the area of the dunes, following a route from Daylight Pass to Townes Pass, has caused the formation of what he termed modified sub-barchan (crescent shaped) dunes.

Another little known fact about sand dunes is they can hold a tremendous amount of water. Although the surface is extremely dry and susceptible to

the blowing wind, the interior of the dunes are virtually soaking wet. When it rains the water quickly percolates down through the sand and is held within the dunes. The surface sand acts as an insulator and prevents evaporation, this is why you will find more vegetation than you would typically expect within the sand dune areas.

There are actually six sets of sand dunes within the park boundaries. The most popular set is described above. The Ibex Dunes are near the southern most limit of the Park, between the Ibex and Saddle Peak Hills, and east of Saratoga Springs. Another set of dunes, appropriately called The Dunes, are in the northern end of Panamint Valley. A unique set of dunes; the Eureka Sand Dunes, is in the Eureka Valley. Northwest of the Eureka dunes is another set of "dunes" made up of sand blown against the mountains that form the west side of the Eureka Valley. Lastly there is a small set of dunes to the north of Salt Lake, on the western edge of Saline Valley. All the sand dunes within the park are closed to vehicles.

The dunes in northern Panamint Valley can be seen by looking north from Highway 190, at the junction with Panamint Valley Road. These dunes are near the middle of the valley, at the base of the mountains. The dunes can be reached by a dirt road 4.8 miles east of Panamint Springs Resort on Highway 190. Drive north on this road for 6 miles; park your vehicle, being careful of the deep gully on the right. The dunes are about three miles west of where you can park. These seldom visited dunes are at the end of a three mile hike. I have found these sand dunes provide an excellent opportunity for the purist that wants to photograph dunes without human foot prints.

The Eureka Sand Dunes are host to a species of dune grass that grows only on those dunes and a small beetle that is found nowhere else in the world. These dunes have been designated a National Natural Landmark and were protected from vehicle traffic years before the area was included in the national park. The Eureka dunes are reported to be the largest set of dunes in the United States, with the main dune reaching 700 feet high. The sand dunes are sometimes referred to as "singing dunes." When a gentle wind is blowing across the higher dunes you can hear a soft humming created by the moving sand. Exploring these dunes is fun, but trying to reach the top of the highest dune takes a lot more time and effort than you may want to spend.

These dunes can be reached by driving west on Big Pine Road from the paved road to Ubehebe Crater. After driving 33½ miles on this washboard, dusty, dirt road you will turn south onto the Eureka Valley Road

Eureka Valley

for 10 more miles. An easier but somewhat longer ride is to approach the Eureka Dunes by driving east from Big Pine. Just north of the town is Highway 168, take this east a short distance to Death Valley Road. This road is paved for most (27½ miles) of the way. You will still have about 19 miles of smooth, but dusty, dirt road to traverse. Camping is permitted at the dunes. There is a single chemical toilet and a few tables, but no water is available.

Another set of dunes is located on the western edge of Saline Valley just north of the normally dry Salt Lake on Saline Valley Road. These dunes are located 43 road miles north on Saline Valley Road from Highway 190. The Saline Valley Road junction is 69.1 miles west of Furnace Creek Ranch. The first 14 miles of this road are mostly paved, but be prepared for some major potholes. In early 1995, this road was being maintained (graded) by Inyo County road crews. I found the road could be easily traversed by a passenger car. This road does go all the way through Saline Valley and connects with Death Valley Road.

Photography in any of the sand dune areas can be challenging. During clear, windless (not too likely) days, the light reflections are at their maximum since sand particles are composed mostly of quartz. However, with the proper selection of filters, film and shutter speed, better than average photos may be taken. There are several times of the day when dune photography is most rewarding. My favorite sand dune shot was taken from the top of the hill on the entrance road to Grotto Canyon, just to the south of the Death Valley dune area, at about five in the afternoon. At this hour the sun is low and orange in color as it strikes the dunes, accentuating their high and low profiles. Although the dunes are over a mile away from this vantage point, good composition can capture the dunes as a foreground with Mesquite Flat and the eastern mountain range as a backdrop.

Cautiously walking the dunes in daylight (sidewinder snakes are not uncommon, although rarely seen) can result in excellent photos of trails and tracks of the nocturnal desert animals. These types of pictures are generally best in very early morning where, with a little luck, you might have a confrontation with a long-tailed lizard, or even a Kangaroo Rat.

The sand dunes flooded in moonlight are exceptionally photogenic. The moonlight photographer in Death Valley is fortunate in having a usually smog-free, cloud free atmosphere in which to work and, consequently, more unobstructed light from the moon. You may want to try waiting quietly, partially concealed by the crest of a dune, to capture the nocturnal wildlife around one of the many clumps of shrubs within the dunes. Do be advised that the Sand Dune Picnic Area is a Day Use Area. You do not want your car to get locked in when the Rangers close the gates.

The perimeter of the sand dunes will allow the watchful nature enthusiast an opportunity to capture views of various desert shrubs and their "sand shadows." The thicker and lower to the ground the shrub is, the more pronounced the shadow becomes. The windward side of an obstacle in the path of the wind-driven sand is generally piled high with sand. At the rear of the obstacle the sand may form one long shadow. In the early stages of development there will be two "ears" or shadows on either side of the plant. The shape and size of the shrub will determine the shape and size of the sand shadow, and there are at least as many of these in various forms as there are sand dunes. I did find some excellent examples of sand shadows near the Eureka Dunes and The Dunes in Panamint Valley.

The shapes and area covered by the dunes is constantly changing. The dunes within Death Valley provide many different photographic and exploring opportunities to visitors that choose to return year after year or even years later. I once met a student from Japan who was mapping the dunes as part of her university thesis. As she discovered the phenomenon of constant and significant change, she found she was confronted with a completely new problem in trying to explain it.

The Salt Pan

Geologists have determined that the entire length of Death Valley, at one time or another, was under water. In many areas of the Valley evidence of these prehistoric bodies of water remain on the rocks. Some of the best examples are at the Badlands at Zabriskie Point, and Shoreline Butte and on the low hills on the way to Keane Wonder Mill. The drying of the lakes coupled with scarcity of rainfall and excessive evaporation has resulted in the formation of the salt flats.

The development of the Death Valley salt pan can be described in geologic periods:

Late Pleistocene: (about 1 million years ago): The valley was filled by a lake estimated to be six hundred feet deep. This provided considerable moisture for the environment and supports the theory of a tropical forest existing in the area of Titus Canyon.

Early Recent: (about 25,000 years ago): The Death Valley of this period was reportedly dryer than now, and the final drying of the lake probably deposited a salt crust zone pretty much like the present one.

Late Recent: (about 2,000 years ago): This period finds Death Valley wetter than now and flooded by a lake 30 feet deep. As the ponds and lake dried up, a salt zone, much like what we see today, was produced. Springs that fed the ponds deposited the sulfates. Flooding and evaporation of the ponds impregnated the carbonate zone with sodium chloride.

Devil's Golf Course is a playa of sorts. It is the approximate bottom of the now dry Lake Manly and it does periodically flood. It starts 6 miles south of Furnace Creek Ranch and continues for 10 miles. The crystalline structures of sodium chloride (table salt) lie in a scattered array of sharp pinnacles, which contradict its designation as a salt flat. Having had the opportunity to stumble and slosh across its vastness on more than one occasion, I can safely state that it is neither flat nor dry.

Salt "Waves" On Central Salt Flat

The water on the salt flat is provided by underground streams; as this water drains into the valley it dissolves salts and other minerals along the way. During the rare rains that fall directly upon the Devil's Golf Course, water erodes and carves the spines on the strange formations on the surface. This surface water then mixes with the salty ground water. Then as this water pools, it combines with the dirt, sand, and clay, and as it evaporates it leaves behind salt and mud structures we see today. This explains why some of the salt pinnacles are white, but most are dirt-colored due to the mixture of mud and salt.

A walk across Devil's Golf Course is an experience that should not be missed, but proceed cautiously as a fall could be very painful. In the warmer months of spring, the crystal texture of the salt pinnacles gives off sounds of tinkling, not unlike breaking glass or pottery when broken or disturbed. Early in the morning following a cloudy and cool day, you may get close to the pinnacles and hear the delicate sounds as the warming sun expands the crystals. Early in spring, many salt pools adorn the surface of the flats and, through their waters, the stark white basins can be seen.

One of the more absorbing pastimes overlooked by many visitors is close observation of the patterned ground within Death Valley's 200 square miles of saltpan. These patterns are not those normally seen from the heights of Dante's View. The patterned ground of the saltpan that you can easily walk upon changes as slowly as geologic time. Evidence of this change may be seen in the 20-Mule Team tracks still faintly visible across the Devil's Golf Course not more than 10 miles south of Furnace Creek. The slowness of change is proven by the fact that the tracks were made in the late 1880s!

The salt patterns have many configurations, but basically have three distinct forms; a polygonal pattern, salt saucers, and salt blisters. The polygonal patterns are more common in the northern salt pan above Furnace Creek and are usually found at the outer edges of the flats. Examples may be seen on the way to the Borax Haystacks on the perimeter of the many salt pools and in the washes in the area. The polygons have raised edges caused by heavier salt deposits in cracks in the mud swelling up to create a border. Inside the polygon is a perfectly flat, pure white, thin coating of salt crystals. More examples of these polygons may be seen just north of the low hills, near the Devil's Cornfield south of Highway 190.

Salt saucers are not too common and not as easy to locate. The western edge of the Devil's Golf Course contains a few wave-like saucers, which are the result of wedges of salt forming in cracks between the segments of the crystallized surface. These large dish-shaped formations have curled up edges formed by salt crusts riding atop the growing wedges of salt. Over time, the wedges continue to grow forcing the surface material into more pronounced saucer formations.

The salt blisters are very common and may be found almost anywhere on the saltpan from the center on out to the edge. These appear as blisters on the ground and are actually small mounds of crusted sand or mud. They are formed by accumulations of salt in the surface layers of the mud. The salt particles, bound together by moisture in the mud, are raised up in solidified mounds as the water evaporates.

A rare formation is the salt cone. These are usually small hollow growths, 3 to 4 inches in height, found in dried salt pools on the Devil's Golf Course. Locating these requires searching the depressions between the salt pinnacles well away from the heavily traveled areas. The salt cones are very delicate and are usually recognized after they have begun to break apart.

Salt Cone At Devil's Golf Course

37

Highs and Lows

Telescope Peak, in the Panamint Range, is the highest point in Death Valley National Park with an elevation of 11,049 feet. The peak is immediately west of Badwater and provides an excellent backdrop for photographs of the salt pool at -279 feet.

To reach the peak, a trail winds its way for 7 miles to the summit from Mahogany Flat Campground (8,133 feet) at the top of Wildrose Canyon. Along the way, near the crest, some fine examples of Limber, Pinyon, and Bristlecone pines are found. Climbing the peak in winter is not recommended unless you are an experienced mountain climber and can provide rope, crampons, ice ax, and the necessary know-how. I recommend that you check-in with the Wildrose Ranger Station before your trip.

Ideally, the latter part of May is best for this trip. Wild flowers are still blooming on the mountain slopes and the heat haze from the valley below is not yet strong enough to obscure the view. The trail is classified as moderately strenuous, but is completely safe for young and old alike, if adequate time is allowed. Average time for the climb is around 6 to 8 hours, with older folks and inexperienced hikers taking a little longer. Plan to leave for the climb just before the sun rises, and you will have plenty of time and light for photography and sightseeing. A trail snack of sweets, nuts, raisins, and the like will make the trip more pleasant and successful. Keep in mind that even strong, healthy walkers may have difficulty with the availability of oxygen as the altitude increases.

In the first mile you will gain about 700 feet elevation and pass the north fork of the Hanaupah Canyon off to your left. In another mile you will have gained another 800 feet and can look up 400 feet to your right at Rogers Peak (9,994 feet). The next mile or so becomes a little easier as you pass through Arcane Meadows and move around 9,980-foot Bennett Peak. About 4 more miles and 1,400 feet of elevation gain will bring you to the top of Death Valley's monarch, Telescope Peak.

At the opposite end of the elevation scale of Death Valley is Badwater. Prior to the 1950's, Badwater was thought to be the lowest point in the United States at 279 feet below sea level. A survey party from the U.S. Geological Survey mapped the area and located two separate points that measured 282 feet below sea level. One point is located about a half a mile west by southwest of the Natural Bridge access road and 3 miles north by northwest from Badwater. The other low point is 4 miles west by northwest of Badwater almost centered between West Side Road and Badwater Road.

The present site of Badwater has a paved parking and turning area, complete with stone steps down to the shallow pool. High above on the mountainside to the east of this site (behind you, if you are facing the pool) is a large white sign with black lettering proclaiming "Sea Level." Directly above the sign at about 6,000 feet is the overlook at Dante's View.

The pool at Badwater is home to an endemic species of desert snail with the Latin name of *Asiminea infirma*. You might chance to find one in or around the roots of saltbrush or iodine bush. I have not had the good fortune to locate these little wonders of the Valley, even with expert help from a graduate biology student from the University of Nevada, the salt-loving invertebrate remained in hiding. These small animals live near the edge of the pool and are quite small making them difficult to see. Most likely you will only succeed in smashing them and their habitat as you look for them. Perhaps it's best just to know they exist, and not risk killing them while attempting to see them.

Badwater

Weather

The weather statistics for the Death Valley area are maintained by the National Park Service at a National Weather Service station behind the Visitor Center. During the early years between 1911 and 1934, weather records were kept by the Greenland Ranch (the former name of Furnace Creek Ranch). This task was taken over by the Park Service around 1935 soon after Death Valley was established as a National Monument.

Southern California Edison, in cooperation with the National Park Service, is now collecting weather data at three locations in the park. The weather data collection stations have been set up at Badwater, Rogers Peak (near Telescope Peak), and the Visitor Center. A computerized graphic display has been set up in the lobby of the Visitor Center so anyone can obtain real-time weather information at a glance.

It has long been an accepted fact that Death Valley is the hottest and driest area in the United States. It has an average annual precipitation of 1.84 inches, a maximum air temperature of 134 degrees (1913), and a ground temperature high of 201 degrees (1972). The high summer (June through September) temperatures are caused by a combination of convection, radiation, and re-circulation of air within the narrow, deep basin. Warm air in the Valley expands and rises to meet cooler air above. The heavier cool air pushes down into the Valley to compress the warm air layers radiating from mountain walls. This constant re-circulation and compression creates heat.

According to National Park Service precipitation records for an 83-year period (1911-1994), the wettest months are November through February. The heaviest annual precipitation 4.54 inches was recorded in 1913 and 1982. In 1929 and 1953 it did not rain at Furnace Creek Ranch during either of these years. The wettest month in Death Valley history was January 1995 with 2.59 inches of rain; this more than made up for the 0.56 inch of rain for all of 1994.

When discussing weather statistics of the Death Valley region, you must realize that the figures quoted relate only to that area which is below sea level, and do not apply to the Park overall. If you consider the rain and snow occurring in the mountainous portion of the Park, the average precipitation would rise to 4 or 5 inches annually. As for temperature, it

Month	Avg Temp	Highest	Lowest	Rain (In.)
January	51.8	87	15	0.24
February	59.0	97	27	0.33
March	66.6	102	30	0.24
April	75.9	111	35	0.12
May	85.0	120	42	0.07
June	94.7	128	49	0.03
July	101.6	134	52	0.11
August	99.1	127	65	0.12
September	90.4	120	41	0.11
October	76.8	113	32	0.09
November	61.9	97	24	0.19
December	52.3	86	19	0.19
Annual	**76.3**	**134**	**15**	**1.84**

National Park Service

is likely that the 83-year average of 76.3 degrees annually for the Valley would drop to about 63.6 degrees for the Park.

Humidity is typically low in the Valley, and is a very influential element to the workings of the human body. As a visitor to this low desert during the warmer seasonal periods, you should respect the fact that low humidity will greatly increase your perspiration rate with a minimum of physical activity. Since the air in the valley is much drier than most of us are used to, you may not realize just how much you are sweating. The dryness of the air will keep your clothing from becoming damp and sticky.

Keep in mind is that most of the people who have "passed on" in the valley have been victims of the dryness rather than the heat. Replacing your water losses continually is a mandatory to survival. Should you become thirsty, remember that thirst is the first sign of dehydration. Drink plenty of liquids while in the Valley, whether you feel the need or not so in order to maintain water equilibrium – a balance between the perspiration losses and the liquid ingested. Also understand that alcoholic beverages and softdrinks are not a substitute for ever important water. It's a good idea to keep a supply of fresh water, about 1 gallon per person, in your car while traveling around the Valley.

Visitors traveling from Furnace Creek to Scotty's Castle will experience an elevation change of 3,100 feet which will make a marked difference in temperature, humidity, and the clothing worn. As a rule of thumb, temperatures will decrease 3 to 5 degrees Fahrenheit for every 1,000 feet of elevation gained. Precipitation and humidity also increase with the gain in elevation.

For a hiker air temperature information is not as valuable as ground temperature data. If you are planning to do some walking in a canyon or on the flats, add 40 to 50 percent to the air temperature readings. You will then know how much heat your feet will be subjected to during the trip. Some hikers carry a small chef's thermometer, to measure air and ground temperature. While walking in the valley, consider the predicament the flowers, shrubs, and animals are in; they must constantly survive the extreme ground temperatures to which we humans pay little or no attention.

Other Desert Terrain

"Gargoyles," rock structures which look like figures carved out of stone, are readily apparent in and around the Kit Fox Hills. These formations are caused by wind erosion cutting away the softer material leaving a ped-

Gargoyles In The Kit Fox Hills

estal of sandstone or shale supporting a harder material at the top or outer edges. When most of the softer material is concentrated towards the center of the rock structure the erosion may create a natural arch such as can be seen in Telephone Canyon, near Emigrant Canyon.

Two types of rock terrain normally escape the visitor that stays "captive" in a vehicle are desert pavement and desert varnish. Desert pavement is predominant in relatively level areas where strong gusts of wind may be frequent. Small stones or pebbles are seen laid out smooth and nearly level as if someone had deliberately set each stone in place. This paving is caused by the wind, which removes the smaller particles of sand from around the pebbles. As the pebbles settle more sand is exposed to be blown away. Eventually, the pebbles have their sand bases removed a little at a time and settle to a depth, or layer, of about one pebble thick.

Be careful when you attempt to get a close-up look at Desert Pavement. There is a small plant, usually smaller than a dime, that grows among the pebbles of the pavement. This is the Spiny Chorizanthe, when the plant is dried, its usual state, the spines are hollow and tend to break off after they enter your skin.

Spiny Chorizanthe

Desert varnish is a common phenomena in desert mountains and hills, and is a reddish-brown, reflective coating seen from a distance if the sun is at the right angle. This coating, or patina, is made up of traces of iron or manganese, worked upon by sun and rain to create a thin film across the exposed surface of the rock. The length of time required to create this coating seems to vary with each geologist or scientist, and I have heard it range from 2 years to 2,000 years. Some excellent examples of desert varnish can be seen along Scotty's Castle road, south of Mesquite Springs Campground. In the late afternoon the rocks will take on a very distinctive reddish, brown glow in the sunlight.

Chapter 3
For the Nature of It

Flora

At the right time and place, the flora of Death Valley can match those seen in the Cascades or Sierras – not in profusion, perhaps, but certainly in beauty. The plants of Death Valley have a lot in common with other plants of the world. They require water and an environment to spread their seeds. They have the ability to adapt to certain changes in their environment for survival. Some desert plants go into a semi-dormant state when moisture becomes scarce. The seeds of many desert flowers are born in a season of plentiful moisture, but will not germinate until conditions are again ideal for them to complete their life cycle and create more seeds.

Among the more common plants to be found without leaving the roadside are the Burroweed, Creosote Bush, Desert Holly, Desert Trumpet, Mesquite, and Turtleback. Turtleback is found in profusion on the shoulders of the highway south of Furnace Creek. It is a compact, low-growing plant with thick, wool-covered leaves. Small yellow blooms appear on the

Desert Trumpet - *Eriogonum inflatum*

Turtlebacks between March and June; if the flowers give off a fragrance, it is hard to detect with the natural pungent odor of the plant filling the air. In the evening primrose family, Death Valley gives you a choice of two colors – the yellow blooms of the common Primrose, and the white-flowering Desert Primrose. Typical of the primrose plants, the flowers "age" on their stems, usually overnight. The white Desert Primrose will age to pink by morning, and the Evening Primrose almost to red.

The Desert Holly, Creosote Bush, and Mesquite probably outnumber all the other Valley plants. Desert Holly is a small shrub with gray-green, holly-like leaves which turn whiter, as the plant forms salt crystals on its leaves in the heat of summer to reduce the plant's moisture usage. Due to this shrub's tolerance to a salty or alkaline environment, the bitter leaves, white flowers, and berry-like fruit keep it out of the edible plant class. Desert Holly can range from 5 shrubs per acre in lower, dryer elevations to almost 250 shrubs per acre in the wetter, northern portion of the Valley.

The Creosote Bush is more widely distributed throughout the Valley than most other plants. The Creosote Bush may be found growing almost anywhere in the Park above sea level, and is a loose, thin plant having small yellow flowers. Despite the Creosote Bush's tall, lean, and lanky form, the small amount of shade that it does supply may satisfy your needs during a break on a hot hike. The Creosote Bush does not have any linkage with the well known wood preservative; however after a rain shower it does give off a slight odor that reminds many of us of creosote oil. Creosote Bush Desert, along the road from Grapevine Ranger Station to Ubehebe Crater, is one of the best places to see the plants, here the density of the shrub probably approaches 125 plants per acre. In the much drier environment of southern Mesquite Flat the Creosote Bush density drops to 2 or 3 shrubs per acre.

The Mesquite has long flowing pods of yellow flowers two to three inches in length, and the plant is armed with long, stiff, and sharp spines. This tree can be found growing out of sand hillocks and in the middle of veritable wastelands. The Mesquite was a food source for the Indians of the Valley; the honey sweet Mesquite Beans were even traded among the Indians families and tribes of the area. Mesquite also had a part in the borax industry of the area. The wood was used in the boiler fires at Harmony Borax Works. Some excellent examples of Mesquite can be found between Triangle Spring and Midway Well on both the east and west sides of Scotty's Castle Road.

Two plants commonly seen and frequently asked about are members of the Eriogonum family. They are the Rixford Eriogonum and the Desert Trumpet plant. The Rixford Eriogonum is normally found at elevations above 1,000 feet, and is often seen in canyons and washes growing to about 18 inches in height. The plant is most often a deep rust-color and looks much like miniature versions of the trees found on the African Veldt. The layered branchlets may sometimes be green if adequate rain has fallen. The Desert Trumpet plant is found at the same elevation, but in larger quantities than the Rixford Eriogonum. This plant is easily recognized by its swollen joints near the head of the plant, and may be green during a wet year and pure white when dried. The name came from the fact that the ends of the branches fan out into the shape of a trumpet.

Rixford Eriogonum

The flowering season in Death Valley can vary, beginning as early as the middle of February and continuing into the month of May. The timing and length of the season are dictated by the amount of rain that has been available and the time of year it happened. With three inches of rain in the Valley by December, it would be difficult to walk anywhere above 500 feet without bumping into flowers in late March. Occasionally, pre-season blooming occurs if moisture and weather conditions are just right for that particular plant's seed. In November 1976, following heavy rains during September, many flowering plants prematurely burst into blossom in the canyons.

Some of the flowers to look for that are easily sighted, even if you are not inclined to leave your vehicle, are the Desert Gold, Purple Phacelia, Gravel Ghost, and Sand Verbena. The Desert Gold, a monstrous sun-flower, can be found blooming all over the fans in the Valley. The Gravel Ghost is a delicate, white flowered plant growing to almost three feet tall. It was so named because of the plant's unusually long single stem with the flower perched on the top. Growing thinly in washes and canyons, the slightest breeze gives the plant a ghostly appearance as the flower seems to dance unsupported in the air.

Many visitors confuse the two purple-flowered plants, Purple Phacelia and Sand Verbena. The Purple Phacelia is an upright plant, growing to about 12 inches with masses of purple flowers. The Sand Verbena is a flat grower commonly seen along the Park roads from sea level on up.

A couple of unusual plants you should look for are the Desert Five-Spot and the mini-flowered Desert Star. The Desert Five-Spot is a tall, basal-leafed, branchless plant topped by multiple stems bearing pale violet flow-ers. Each of the five petals of the flower bears a crimson spot on the in-side base. The petals of the flower usually remain in a semi-closed posi-tion, so it is necessary to gently blow the petals outward to view the crim-son blotches. The Desert Star is a tiny plant with equally tiny blossoms that look like miniature sunflowers, and are as big around as a pencil eraser. The flowers may appear singly or in a cluster and take some searching to locate. They are a typical "belly flower" – you will have to get your stomach to the ground to find the first few.

Death Valley is also host to numerous types of vegetation that puzzle the average visitor, or appear to be out of place and are not explained in other publications. Visitors generally inquire about the large trees spread around the Furnace Creek area and bordering the hotel at Stovepipe Wells Village. These are Tamarisk trees native to the Mediterranean area. The Tamarisk was introduced to Death Valley around the 1890s.

Mesquite was more plentiful in the Valley prior to the introduction of the Tamarisk trees. These trees were planted as wind breaks and for shade, but their tremendous appetite for water and indestructible nature, has reduced the Mesquite growth in many areas. This is most evident at the mouth of Furnace Creek Wash, which reportedly was a veritable garden of Mesquite. Now about all you see there are Tamarisk and Date Palm trees.

Date Palm trees can be readily accepted in a desert environment, but the 1,800 palms at Furnace Creek Ranch will make a newcomer very inquisitive. Originally about 120 trees were planted here in about 1925 by the Department of Agriculture, to obtain pest free nursery stock. Now they contribute to the oasis that has been created in the area. The dates are harvested for sale, and to make date-nut bread for Furnace Creek Inn and Ranch and for public sale at the General Store.

Even stranger than Date Palms and Tamarisk trees is a destructive parasite called Dodder. The first thing that will attract your attention is the color; Dodder is orange. While driving through the northern portion of Mesquite Flat towards Scotty's Castle, you might notice Dodder as a large bunch of grass-like material covering a native plant. Dodder is a parasite which attaches itself to healthy plants and leaches out the moisture it needs. This parasite is so effective at pulling moisture out of the host plant that it feels damp when you touch it. Dodder is usually found in the springtime, during the flower season, and is carried from plant to plant by the wind.

A little known fact about Death Valley National Park is its collection of endemic plants. These are plants that grow nowhere else in the world. The Park is particularly suited for an array of such plants due to its extreme environment and unique terrain. The most recent count of endemic plants in Death Valley is 20 and this accounts for only those that occur within the Park boundaries.

Valley Cacti

There are relatively few, if any, cacti found below sea level in the Valley. For that matter, you might have difficulty finding cacti below 1,000 feet elevation. The three most common cactus plants, Beavertail, Cholla, and Cottontop, are frequently found on the higher ground of Mesquite Flat, the hills of Titus Canyon and other high canyons. They are also found throughout the areas of the various passes in and around the Valley.

Beavertail cactus is characterized by large, flat, fleshy pads or leaves that are olive drab to gray in color. As is the case with most of the cacti in the area, the blooming time of the Beavertail runs from March to May and sometimes into June. In proportion to the plant the flowers are quite large. They are either a rose or purplish color and grow at the top edges of the leaves. The stems of the Beavertail do not have spines as such, but are covered with short, fine hairs.

The Indians of the early Death Valley discovered that the Beavertail cactus is filled with a sweet sap in early June. The Indians would break off the stems with sticks, rub off the hairy barbs with bunches of grass, and expose the cleaned stems to the sun for drying. When completely dried, they were stored and when needed for food simply boiled and salted.

The anthropologist F. V. Coville, describes another method used by the Indians for preparing the cactus:
"A hole about ten inches in depth and three feet in diameter, is dug in the ground and lined with stones. Upon this a fire is built and other stones thrown in. When they are all thoroughly heated,

the ashes, coal, and all but one layer of stones are scraped away, and some fresh or moistened grass spread in the hole. Next, a layer of cactus joints is added, then more hot stones, and so on until the pile is well rounded. The hole is then covered with sacking (originally with a mat of sedges), and lastly with moist earth. After about twelve hours of steaming, the pile is opened and the Navo, as the cooked cactus is called, is salted and eaten. Prepared as it is, in larger quantities than can be disposed of at once, a portion is dried and preserved. It is then, in texture and appearance, similar to un-peeled dried peaches."

The Cholla is generally found in the same areas as the Beavertail, and is distinguished by its tree-like growth with branchlets in clusters. Similar to other cacti, the flowers appear at the ends of the upper branches, or stems. The flowers are unusual in that they are a waxy green color, from a distance, the Cholla does not look as if it is flowering. Some very fine, young specimens are located near Death Valley Buttes and around the Greenwater area. Be careful when you examine this cactus as it is armed with barbed spines that can be very painful. The heavily spined branch sections are known to break off as their barbs securely anchor themselves to your clothes and to say they are difficult to remove is an understatement.

Another rather commonplace cactus is the Cottontop, a member of the barrel cactus family. The Cottontop designation arose from the puffs of white, cottony-appearing fruits which adorn the tops of the stems in the spring. The plants exhibit a wide assortment of size, color, and shape. I have seen some very large specimens while exploring the mountains above Titus Canyon. The barrels of these cacti were at least a foot larger in diameter and twice as high as Cottontop found in the lower elevations. In the northern part of the Valley, look for smaller plants with 3 to 6 barrels. Depending on the time of year and amount of moisture available to the cactus, the barrels will vary from a stark white to a deep red in color.

Cottontop Barrel Cactus

Driving east along Highway 190 from Stovepipe Wells Village, you will come upon a scene, on both sides of the highway, reminiscent of the Midwest. This is the Devil's Cornfield with hundreds of Arrow Weed plants that look like shocks of corn from a distance. For almost as far as you can see, large shocks of grass, standing up to 10 feet high, grow out of the desert floor. Triangle Spring, 5 miles north, is the source of underground water for the Arrow Weed plants. The base of this large, grass-like plant is sometimes several feet above ground level, resting on it's exposed root system. Their unusual growth form is attributed to a lack of surface moisture, sandy soil, and strong wind. Over time the winds in this area have eroded soil that is not bound together by the roots of these plants. The density of these large plants is about 75 to 100 plants per acre.

Fauna

Survival of the desert animals of Death Valley was accomplished along the same lines as the plants – adaptation. Most of the desert animals are nocturnal and travel for food or water during night-time hours when temperatures are somewhat lower. Larger desert animals seek shelter in caves, crevices, or under whatever brush may be available during the high-temperature hours. The rodent population, including rabbits, are generally found in underground burrows, some almost 18 inches deep, where the temperatures average 50 to 60 percent below those on the surface.

It is unfortunate that the human senses of sight, smell, and hearing are not as keen as that of the desert animals. Because of this, and the fact that most of the desert mammals are nocturnal, the more interesting life forms of the desert escape your view. The Coyote, Kit Fox, and Gray Fox are rarely spotted in the daytime. During a moonlit night, however, glimpses of the Coyote and Kit Fox may be had at the sand dunes or around the mesquite hummocks of Mesquite Flat or Bennett's Well areas. I have seen Kit Fox crossing the salt flat just north of Harmony Borax Works at sunup on two occasions. The Kit Fox is smaller in stature than the coyote, about the size of a small dog with oversized ears and a black-tipped tail. The Gray Fox is more common outside of Death Valley proper, and can be found along the foothills of the eastern Grapevine Mountains in Nevada.

Coyotes are a bit more brazen, I have seen a few during the daytime in the area east of the sand dunes and into Mud Canyon. The Coyote will not be difficult to identify as it normally walks or runs with its tail hung down along its legs. These highly adaptable animals have adjusted to the number of non-threatening human visitors in the park. I remember one trying to play the role of the lonely, hungry dog on the shoulder of the road. Remember, these are wild animals that will bite, do not feed even the cute ones. Another sobering fact is that once fed a Coyote may become a nuisance, and begin "demanding" food from people; in this situation the animal must be destroyed. Don't be indirectly responsible for taking the life of one of these beautiful animals.

The white-tailed Antelope Ground Squirrel and round-tailed ground squirrel are common in the Valley. Although not able to identify it at the time, I had a white-tailed squirrel check out my food supply while camped in the Funeral Mountain foothills. At my campsite there was little or no vegetation, so its appearance was rather surprising. These animals generally frequent Mesquite clumps, where they can feed on plant material.

Although rodents comprise the largest proportion of the desert animal life, they are likely to be the most difficult to find. Since they are, for the most part, burrowing animals, sightings in the heat of the day are rare. During the extreme dryness and high temperatures of summer, the survival of rodents depends on a biological process called aestivation, which is best defined as a summer state of hibernation. This is a semi-dormant state in which body temperature, metabolism, heart rate, and respiration processes are slowed to well below normal. This more than "resting" state reduces the food and water requirements to a minimum until the environment is again suitable for normal activity. The best example is the Kangaroo Rat. Their burrowed dens have been found almost 3 feet deep; and during extremely hot weather the rat will seal off the entrance to conserve moisture and cool air.

Most of the desert rodents obtain their moisture from either the plant materials or insects they eat. It has been proven in scientific tests that the Kangaroo Rat is equipped with some kind of moisture generation system within its small body. Tests concluded that free access to water did not increase its water content, nor did an exclusively dry food diet decrease the water content of the rat's body, (Journal of Cellular Comparative Physiology, 1948, "Water Conservation in Desert Rodents").

No self-respecting Death Valley text would be complete without some mention of the Desert Bighorn Sheep and its major competitor, the Burro. The Burro was introduced into the Valley by prospectors and miners in the late 1800s, and the animals we see today are the descendants of those that were turned loose or simply got away. The Desert Bighorn Sheep, on the other hand, is a true native of this region. The competition between these animals stems from the fact that both animal populations have survived using the same food and water supplies. Today, there are several hundred Desert Bighorn Sheep that are found in the mountains within the boundaries of the park.

The Desert Bighorn Sheep usually avoids contact with humans. I have not been fortunate enough to see one in my 25 plus years of regular visits to the Valley.

Since in some areas the Burro outnumbered the Desert Bighorn Sheep at least three to one, there was a serious wildlife management problem. The Burro population coupled with the differences in foraging, watering and traveling habits; created a significant impact on the ecosystem that was slowly but surely reducing the Desert Bighorn Sheep herd. If left unchanged the situation would have resulted in the eventual total loss of the Desert Bighorn Sheep in this area.

Estimates are that the ideal Burro habitat is 15 square miles per animal. Were the entire 5,189 square miles of the Park considered an acceptable Burro habitat, the Burro population should have realistically been about 350 animals. Rather than deliberately destroy the Burros, the National Park Service has developed a Burro population control program to maintain an acceptable number of Burros in the park. This plan includes participation in the Adopt-a-Burro Program created by the Bureau of Land Management. Complete elimination of the Burro in Death Valley National Park is not part of the plan, but close management of the total population is. I can remember times, before the management of the Burro herds, that it was unsafe to drive at the speed limit through Emigrant Canyon on the way to Wildrose. The Burros were rather substantial obstacles on the road.

Creepy, Crawly Things

Typical of sage and sand country, lizards abound in Death Valley. Your chances of seeing lizards in the Valley are excellent, and none of them are poisonous or dangerous. Perhaps the most hideous looking reptile is the Desert Iguana. The Desert Iguana has been frequently found in the eastern mountain ranges from low to high elevations.

The strangest lizard, and not easy to find, is the Gecko. It is the only lizard capable of making sounds. The body of the Gecko is a reddish-pink that appears to be relatively transparent in the right light. The banded or collared Gecko darts quickly away on all fours when scared; once it has attained enough speed, it concentrates its motive power on its frog-like hind legs.

There are some lizards in the sand dunes area that are quite amusing to watch when they are startled. They will skitter along the surface very rapidly and suddenly dive into the sand, head first. Once under the protection of a layer of sand, they will vibrate their bodies to get deeper and to move away from their point of entry. If you gently disturb the general area above their hiding place, they will not attempt to surface, but will continue to vibrate their bodies deeper and move to another location. Uncovering this lizard results in extreme panic, whereby the lizard will make an escape out of the sand, skitter across the surface for a few feet, and make another dive.

You might have guessed that with all these lizards skittering about, there are bound to be snakes around to control them. The Sidewinder rattlesnake is not uncommon around the Valley. It's usually found in the mesquite-topped hills and in the lower portions of some canyons. The Sidewinder and its big brother, the Panamint Rattlesnake, are poisonous; so try not to walk around barefooted at night as these reptiles are nocturnal. Learn to recognize the Sidewinder and its track for your own safety, if not for your academic interest.

The track of the Sidewinder is easily recognized. It uses an intricate system of segmented plates of muscle that permit it to advance its body, section by section, forming a distinct S-shaped track. The Sidewinder, in this undulating form of locomotion, finds no difficulty in gaining traction over loose sand or smooth places. The Panamint Rattlesnake, found typically at the higher elevations of the Panamint Mountains, employs the caterpillar type locomotion common to most snakes.

During the day, unless it is quite cool, the snakes spend their time resting and hiding from the sun and visitors. Snakes are cold-blooded and do not have heat-regulating systems in their bodies, they resort to any means to conserve or limit their body heat. Since their ideal temperature range is between 70 and 90 degrees, your chances of seeing a sidewinder are not too good during the daylight hours. Although, I usually have been able to find rattlesnakes in the bed of the wash just as you enter Grotto Canyon from the road on the fan.

On the gravel floors of canyons, snakes are usually found curled in a tight coil atop stones matching their body color. Their resting technique in the sandy places is much more subtle, here they will bury their bodies down into the sand with just a small portion of the head and eyes protruding.

Scorpion

More commonly seen around the Valley will be the Chuckwalla, Horned Toad, Scorpion, and Tarantula. The Chuckwalla lizard was on the top of the list of delicacies for the earlier Shoshone, despite its habit of running into a crevice and swelling up to prevent capture. The Desert Horned Lizard or Horned Toad is almost as ugly as the Desert Iguana but considerably smaller. It can be found in sand or gravel covered areas from the low desert to several thousand feet elevation.

Scorpions and Tarantulas frequently seen in the Park are not deadly poisonous, but the Scorpion's sting can leave the affected area swollen and painful for a few days. To avoid unnecessary discomfort in your travels throughout the Valley, exercise care in entering old buildings, climbing rocks, or hiking the sandy places. One particular place to be on the lookout for Scorpions is any of the public restrooms, even in populated areas.

Tarantula

Speaking of discomfort, the few moist areas in the Valley appear to be a favorite place for a particularly vicious species of black fly. Typical locations that attract the fly on warm slightly humid days are along the creek at Furnace Creek, Klare Spring in Titus Canyon, Cottonwood Creek at the end of Cottonwood Canyon, and any of the Mesquite groves along the edge of the salt flats where surface water is in evidence. Fortunately for the full-time residents of Death Valley, there are also about ten species of bats that help control the population of the flies.

An experience worthy of mention concerning an insect was my confrontation with an a Sand Weevil. Many of us have seen beetles come and go and never lifted an eyelid, but an albino beetle? The fact that the creature was white was only part of the surprise. My attention was drawn by its rocking from side to side while moving ahead as if each grain of sand it passed over was a boulder. When I bent down to get a closer look the poor beetle stiffened and rolled over as if it had suddenly died. As I walked to a nearby sand dune, I watched the white blob come to life as my footsteps ceased to be felt, or I was no longer within its range of vision. This creature was playing dead as a survival tactic similar to a chameleon changing color.

Desert Pupfish

Fish in Death Valley? There certainly are! These fishes are called pup-fish and are descendants of a form (*Fundulus*) that were isolated in small streams and spring pockets some 20,000 years ago as the lakes of the Death Valley dried up. According to the Department of Interior's Task Force Report of March 1971, there are "...10 recognized distinct species and subspecies of these fish found in Inyo and San Bernadino Counties in California, and adjacent Nye County in Nevada. They inhabit desert springs, seeps, and streams with each variety confined to a single habitat in most instances." One source has it that the name "pupfish" was given them because they move themselves about by wagging their tails like puppies.

The five types or species and habitat of the pupfish found within Death Valley National Park are:

Species	Habitat
Cyprinodon dabolis	Devil's Hole
Cyprinodon milleri	Cottonball Marsh
Cyprinodon nevadensis amargosae	Amargosa River northwest of Saratoga Springs
Cyprinodon nevadensis nevadensis	Saratoga Springs
Cyprinodon salinus	Salt Creek

The fish vary in length from one to two inches. Pupfish species are found in both fresh and salt water ponds and streams in the desert. Studies have shown that these fish can survive in a wide range of water temperatures and salt concentrations. Research has shown these fish can tolerate water as hot as 112° and as cold as 40°. The Cottonball Marsh Pupfish has been observed alive in water that has five times the salt concentration of normal sea water.

The Devil's Hole Pupfish, is listed as an endangered species. The entire population of this species lives in a single limestone cavern that has a mere 180 square feet of surface water. This is the smallest known habitat of any vertebrate species in the world. These fish actually live on a rock shelf that is just under the surface of the water, and only occupies a portion of the total area.

To more dramatically illustrate the concern for the future of the pupfish, a Desert Fishes Council was formed in 1970, "dedicated to the preservation of America's desert fishes." Its primary aim is to provide active investigation committees to promote the protection and preservation of all desert fishes. This council's efforts have been successful in preserving the pupfish habitat at Devil's Hole. Thus reducing the threat of losing yet another species to "progress."

All the species of pupfish are an important part of Death Valley's history and natural environment. These pupfish are an endemic fish, common only to this area. Once gone, they cannot be replaced.

Perhaps the best and most popular place to see pupfish is Salt Creek, in central Death Valley. The fish are active and visible in the spring (March and April). The boardwalk that follows the main creek provides an excellent point from which to view the fish and ensures minimal disruption of the fish's habitat. If you are not inclined to walk great distances, be assured that I usually find an abundance of fish within ¼ mile of the start of the boardwalk. A Department of the Interior report stated these fishes were aggressive. After watching them for a short time you will agree with the claim these fish are very aggressive. They don't ever seem to tire of chasing each other with more than playing on their minds.

Cottonball Marsh was the site of the most successful borax mining in Death Valley. It is also the home to another of the pupfish species. This

site is approximately 5 miles south of Salt Creek on the west side of the salt flat. It can be reached by either hiking south from the Salt Creek area or by hiking west from Harmony Borax Works. The trek from Harmony could be coupled with a side trip to the Borax Haystacks. I recommend that you wear hiking boots that have been water-proofed for this trip. Stay at the edges of the ponds in this area so as not to significantly impact the pupfish's habitat.

I cannot recommend a visit to Devil's Hole. This remote area is within a large preserve and thus must be protected from uninformed people that might inadvertently fall into the hole and from ever-present vandalism. The hole is surrounded by a chain-link fence with a small viewing platform on one side of the enclosure. There is only a modest wood sign within the enclosure, identifying the site as a home to pupfish. The water is about 25 feet below the surface of the ground and 20 feet below the platform. The opening of the hole itself is approximately 50 feet long and 15 to 20 feet wide at the top, the surface of the water covers about 200 square feet. No one has been able to determine the actual depth of the cavern below this opening. The fish live and breed on a small shelf at one end of the pool and cannot be seen from the viewing platform. At one time the fish in this location were in extreme danger of extinction, but efforts to save them have been successful, and so far their population seems to be increasing.

My visits to the Saratoga Springs and Amargosa River areas have been infrequent, and usually in the fall, so I cannot speak knowledgeably regarding the pupfish viewing at these two locations. Most visitors that do go to this area, usually do so by taking Highway 127 south from Death Valley Junction to the Harry Wade Exit near Tecopa. The other alternative is the winding road past Badwater and then a dirt road, with sometimes deep sand, south of Ashford Mill.

There are also small fish in the streams and irrigation ponds around Furnace Creek Ranch. These are not pupfish. They are Western Mosquitofish. These fish were introduced into these waters to control mosquito and other pest populations.

Chapter 4
Backcountry

Desert Survival

The seemingly unlimited expanse of Death Valley National Park constantly challenges the visitor to be in the right place at the right time to uncover its mysteries. The fortunate ones are those who leave the confines of their vehicles and walk the backcountry exploring canyons, washes and the historic and geologic sites hidden within. Off the main roads of this beautiful desert country its barrenness comes to life and the desolation turns to beauty. You are invited to seek out the wonders that abound here, and your appetite to unlock the Valley's mysteries will become larger in proportion to the number and frequency of your visits.

Leaving the blacktop and venturing on foot, across salt flats, up into canyons, and along the mountain tops in the desert requires a few precautions; one of these is acclimation. Acclimatizing to the Death Valley desert is not only necessary physiologically, but is also of benefit to your psychological well-being. The four most important elements of direct concern to your human welfare are air and ground temperature, humidity,

Hikers At McLean Spring

and terrain. The right combination of these elements without sufficient water and rest can leave you a dehydrated lump in a very short time. The secret to survival is simple; know where you are going, take plenty of water, watch the weather, and let someone else know about the trip.

While in the backcountry, whether on foot or in a vehicle, the Park Service restricts camping to areas at least a mile from a maintained road, or five miles from any established campground. Other necessary restrictions include no collecting of firewood or removal of any objects, and to respect the rights of private claim or land owners within, and immediately beyond, the Park boundary. At the Visitor Center, you may find accurate and friendly information about backcountry trips, and also have an opportunity to register your intended trek for your safety. There is a simple form available that is filled out before you begin the trip and on your return to record the things you have seen as well as road conditions for the benefit of the next traveler. Speaking of road conditions, avoid overrunning the end and sides of the roads as has happened in some areas like Cottonwood Canyon.

Understanding Topographic Maps

To backcountry travelers on foot or in vehicles, a good map is their best companion. A good map is one that has three main features: distance, direction, and symbols. The latter feature describes land elevation, water sources, structures, and roads. A road map from the local service station is of no value in the backcountry as it does not contain all three of these features. A United States Geological Survey quadrangle, or topographic map does. These maps include the vast majority of the data a backcountry traveler may need. If you have never used a topographic map, the following information will decode the map's contents.

Elevation: A topographic map indicates the shape of the land by imaginary lines called contour lines that follow the ground surface to depict elevation. These are printed in brown ink. The change in elevation between contour lines can range from five to 200 feet, being larger for steep, mountainous country, and smaller for flat land. Two kinds of contour lines make elevation calculations simple; an index line which occurs every fourth or fifth line is in heavier print, and supplementary lines which are lighter and depict elevations in gradual steps between the index contours. Figures are printed at intervals along the index contour to identify eleva-

tion. As an example, the majority of maps for the area bounded by the sea level line in Death Valley have 40-foot contour intervals. Every light brown line represents an elevation change of 40 feet, and every fifth line (index contour) represents an elevation of 200 feet. At various points on the topo's, checked and unchecked elevation figures are printed on the map. The measured, checked elevations are printed in black, and the calculated, unmeasured elevations are printed in brown. Using these figures in conjunction with the contour intervals, an accurate determination of elevation, and rate of climb or decent, at any point on the map can be made.

In the field, "bench marks" may also prove invaluable for elevation as well as location. Bench marks are indicted on topographic maps with the letters "BM" immediately followed by an elevation number, all printed in black ink. A bench mark is a rock or concrete ground marker about twelve inches high and topped with a 3½ inch brass plate upon which is engraved the elevation of its location. These bench marks are permanent control points established by the Geological Survey to, "... develop and maintain correct scale, position, and orientation of the map." Be careful in using the bench marks adjacent to the roads in the southern part of the

Park. They have been placed by the Coast and Geodetic Survey, and do not have the elevations inscribed on them. The majority of Geological Survey markers are commonly found about 50 feet off the shoulders of the main highways in the valley.

One cautionary note is that some of the Geologic Survey topographic maps of the valley have their contours and elevations printed in meters. Other maps, also from the Geologic Survey, continue to use feet as the standard unit. Be sure to verify which unit is used on the map you are looking at.

Symbols: All of the symbols utilized in the production of topographic maps are color-coded. The following is excerpted from the Topographic Map Symbol Sheet:

Black is used for man-made or cultural features such as roads, trails, buildings, names, and boundaries.

Blue is used for water or hydrologic features such as lakes, rivers, marshes, and glaciers.

Brown is used for relief or elevation features – land shapes portrayed by contours.

Green is used for woodland cover, with typical patterns to show scrub, and forests.

Red emphasizes important roads, shows built-up urban areas, public land subdivision lines.

It is important that you realize the changing scene with respect to time. Structures can collapse, burn, or be hauled away. Perennial streams may become intermittent and vice versa. Roads may be altered, added, or eliminated. Death Valley and Saline Valley topo's were updated from aerial photographs in the 1980's and have been published as provisional releases; the release date represents the date of the latest photographic material used.

Accuracy: Errors are rarely found on topographic maps. All of the maps published by the Geological Survey must comply to National Map Accuracy Standards. These are: horizontal (distance) accuracy requires 90% of the map points to be within 1/50th of an inch (about 100 feet on the ground), and vertical accuracy (elevation) requires 90% of the contour line interpolations to be correct within ½ of the contour interval.

Scale (distance): At the bottom center of each topo, a scale is provided to determine distances in miles, feet, and kilometers. When measuring distances to be traveled using the map and associated scale, remember that the topo is a flat projection of the actual area. Trails and roads traversing steep elevations will add to your total calculated mileage. Also found at the bottom center of most topo's is the contour interval in feet or meters. This stated interval denotes the elevation between the supplementary (light brown) contour lines.

Declination: On the bottom left-hand side of a topographic map is text denoting Magnetic North Declination, the difference that exists between true north and magnetic north. Since magnetic north is situated about 1,000 miles from the North Pole, and all topo's are oriented to the North Pole; the declination allows you to correct for the difference between your compass reading and the map. The topo's of Death Valley have a declination between 14°30' to 15°30' east (read as degrees and minutes). A simple method is to use a straight edge to draw the magnetic lines right on the map using the declination as a guide to set the angle from the true north. Draw as many lines as you will need to cover the area of your travels. When in the field you need only align your lines with the compass needle to account for the declination. Of course you could get one of the new micro-processor based compasses and put an end to all the messing around.

Obtaining Topo's: Most well-equipped hiking, skiing, and mountain supply stores carry topo's. In Death Valley, topo's are available at the Visitor Center. You may also write to the nearest Geological Survey Distribution Center and request an index to order the topo's direct. An index of topographic maps for California is available from the U. S. Geologic Service. The Death Valley National Park recreational map, published by Tom Harrison Cartography, is dated 1994 and provides an excellent reference for identifying the features and attractions of the Park. This map is available through Rand McNally Map and Travel Stores.

The U. S. Geological Survey has been busy updating most of the maps that cover the park. In the process they have determined that a 7.5 minute quadrangle is the best suited format for this area. Each 7.5 minute map covers an area of approximately 7 miles by 8½ miles, the scale on these maps is 1 inch equals 24,000 or 1 inch equals 2000 feet.

Water and Water Caches

Although most of us differ slightly psychologically, physiologically, and metabolically, there is a common ailment afflicting visitors to the Valley – THIRST! When in the mountains, Sierras or Cascades, I occasionally take a drink of water to rinse away the residue of a dusty trail. However, in the desert my water consumption rate is at least two quarts every 10 miles. You may need more or less but the secret is to drink water often, do not wait for signs of thirst. Thirst is the first warning sign of dehydration. Do not rely on alcohol or soft drinks to replace the fluid in your body, they are simply not effective and may actually work against their intended purpose.

This desert is not like the Mohave with 4-6,000 feet elevations. Death Valley has 550 square miles at or below sea level and the humidity is almost always low. The combinations of high temperature, low humidity, and the ground heat work together to draw the moisture out of your system. As I've said before, most of the people who have died in this desert have been victims of the dryness, not the heat. When you put water into your system in amounts equal to the losses from perspiration plus a bit extra for internal functions, everything is rosy. If you do not replace that which was lost, or replace it at a lower rate than your perspiration rate,

An Open Water Cache

you will gradually dehydrate. At somewhere between 15% and 22% dehydration, you will die. Equally important as the quantity is the water temperature at the time it is ingested. The theory is that your perspiration rate will be reduced at some proportionate amount relative to how far below your body temperature the drinking water temperature lies.

Some people feel compelled, when in the desert, to supplement their water intake with salt tablets. If you are one of those, consult you doctor prior to simply throwing the salt pills in with your gear. Perhaps you will find that your particular make-up calls for electrolytic fluids rather than simple salt. If in doubt, just plain water is usually the best all around weapon against dehydration.

Despite the fact that there are over 400 streams, springs, and seeps in the Death Valley region, most are not dependable. The cache and carry water method is under your direct control and, properly administered, will prevent you from becoming a statistic. Carry at least one gallon of water per person per day, and use soft, plastic bottles whether they are in your pack or in your vehicle.

Water for caches is the next concern, soft, strong, polyethylene one-gallon bottles with screw tops are the safest for your lifeline. Before you simply start setting out caches, carefully plan your route. Use topographic maps to determine the approximate location for each planned cache. **Then, get approval from the National Park Service, before digging anywhere in the park.**

The physical caching of the water supply is accomplished by preparing a hole at least eighteen inches deep and one-third larger in diameter than the bottles. The cache should contain a minimum of two gallons per person to allow refilling of the personal supply, plus some for cooking, washing, or what-ever. The oversize hole will be deep enough to keep your water cool and fresh, discourage possible disturbances from animals, and provide a workable soil area around the bottles to expedite their future removal. Place the bottles level and tightly against each other at the base of the hole. A three-foot stake is stuck between the center gap of the bottles, and loose sand or gravel poured into the gap to set the stake in place. Fill the hole with as much loose, small sand and gravel as available, and keep larger material for last.

Water caches should not be any further apart than one day's travel, be conservative when determining how far you can travel in the allotted time. The caches you set out should be marked on your topo's which describe the route of your intended trip. After ten days or so in the backcountry, the mind has a tendency to go blank. If you are walking up into canyons that are unfamiliar to you, they begin to look alike after a while. It's not impossible to find a half-dozen ledges where you thought your water was cached. When two or more persons are traveling together, it is a good idea for everyone to know the exact location of caches in the event of separation or accident. One more precaution – when caching your water supply, try to do so with as little ceremony as possible and as much secrecy as permissible. The cache is your lifeline, but curiosity seekers do not always understand that, and might come by after you leave and turn your water cache inside out.

Remember, at the end of your trip, go back and remove your stakes and bottles.

Hiking and Backpacking

This section will explore the four possible ways a hiker may take advantage of seeing Death Valley: summer hiking, day hikes, backpacking, and the Big Trek (walking the length of the Valley). To safely and sanely accomplish any of these, the potential walker should have a look at some equipment essentials which are basic survival techniques in this low desert.

The pack, frame, clothing, and food used on a desert trek is a personal choice, determined by the hiker regardless of his or her desert experiences. My particular selection of these items is based upon well over 2,500 miles of Death Valley hiking, and they have proven to work best for me. One item of critical importance often overlooked when hiking the Valley is shelter. Two elements that dictate the need for this shelter are wind and sun. A simple, light, and economical shelter may be constructed from a "space" blanket. A good space blanket costs about $15, and is about 5 x 7 feet. It consists of a insulating filler, coated on one side with a silver reflective material, and the other side is red or blue to collect solar heat.

Used as a lean-to sun shelter, the light and heat reflecting qualities of the space blanket will reduce the air temperature around you by up to 15 de-

grees. The loose soil composition, in those areas fit to rest your body, will normally not accept and hold tent stakes. The ground side of the lean-to may be adequately secured by a couple of large rocks placed at the corners. Inexpensive, take-down tent poles will support the front edge if tied off with nylon cord to large rocks placed at a 45 degree angle from the shelter corners. If used as a wind and sand shelter, double up on the number and size of rocks placed on the ground edge.

Another beat-the-heat trick to accompany your sun shelter is the use of an air mattress. Though adding extra weight, it is the most satisfactory ground cloth on two counts – comfort and insulation. Resting on an air mattress places the body 4 to 6 inches above the surface of the ground where the air is cooler. Always make sure to lay out a ground covering for the air mattress to protect it from abrasion and puncture.

Summer Hiking: Both the Park Service and I have made every effort to discourage summer hiking in Death Valley. The months of June through September in the Valley are drenched in high temperatures (95-120 degrees), low humidity, and on occasion, heavy and destructive rainstorms. The calculated risk of hiking under these conditions is best left to the military and their desert survival projects. Should you not be easily discouraged, contact the Park Service Headquarters at Furnace Creek and place before them all the data you have in the way of routes, schedules, and distances to be traveled. You will find the Park Rangers cooperative and informative, but they must determine if you are fit for such a trek and will impose their policies on summer hiking, which are:

1) Arrive several days prior to the hike and spend time adjusting to the temperatures and learning the country.
2) Plan a route to follow along open roads, where a support party can provide assistance; many of the dirt roads are closed during the summer. Plan the hiking party to consist of at least two people with an additional person in a vehicle to follow hikers' progress and supply their needs.
3) File an itinerary and a map of your route with the Chief Ranger's office prior to starting your hike.

Much of this may not thwart you from an intended summer trek of the Valley, and you might even convince yourself that an air temperature of 120 degrees is comfortable if the humidity is low. But try convincing your feet that the 180 degrees they are wading through is also comfortable!

Hikers At Surveyor's Well

Day Hikes: Although much less complex than a summer hike or a back-pack trek, the day hike should be approached with the same precautions. Water caches are not necessary, but always have more than an adequate supply on your person. Check in with the Park Service if you are not sure of the hike route, and tell someone where you are going. The following hikes were selected for their geologic interest, historical significance, or just plain fun. Most are easy to moderate treks under 10 miles in length. The name of the site or area is followed by the topo, elevation, and approximate mileage. When parking your vehicle along the highway, do not drive beyond the graded shoulder.

Borax Haystacks (topo: *Beatty Junction, Furnace Creek, and West of Furnace Creek*, elev:-260', hike: 5.2 miles): This is a fun hike best accomplished at sunrise. You may start out from Harmony Borax Works walking north by northwest, or begin from the Visitor Center building on the trail alongside the building. At certain times of the year this can be a very sloppy walk, so wear old clothes and expect to get your boots caked with mud and salt. There is almost 15 square miles of haystacks on the salt pan. They are piles of borate material which were originally stacked here by Chinese laborers, starting in 1882 until 1888, to prove claim assessment work for Harmony. Large salt pools along the way are not uncommon.

Burned Wagons Point (topo: *Stovepipe Wells NE, and Grotto Canyon*, elev: -120, hike: 5 miles): Drive to the Highway 190 entrance to the Sand Dune Picnic Area and park well off the pavement. On the south side of the highway, opposite the entrance road is a faint dirt track heading south. Hike this track past the Mesquite hummocks and alongside the hills. The Burned Wagons Point sign is mounted on a tall, metal pipe at the foot of the hill to your left (east). This is the location where, in 1849, the Jayhawkers burned their wagons, slaughtered and smoked some of their oxen. From here, they started their walk out of the valley over what is now Townes Pass and Jayhawker Canyon. Bring water. Head south to the base of the jutting cliff to see the waterfall, near McLean Spring and the ponds created by the surfacing of Salt Creek.

Cottonball Marsh (topo: *Beatty Junction*, elev: -267, hike: 11 miles): This marsh is located approximately 5 miles south of Salt Creek on the western edge of the salt flat. You can either hike south from the Salt Creek parking area, or hike west from Highway 190 at the turn off for the

Salt Pinnacles Near Cottonball Marsh

National Park Service (NPS) Residential Area. The distance from the highway to the marsh is also five miles and will bring you very close to the Borax Haystacks. This is the marsh where Aaron and Rosie Winters discovered borax in 1881. On the west side of the marsh you will find the site of the Westside Borax Camp. The marsh is 2½ miles long from north to south and is about a mile across at its widest point. The water in the marsh is 12-18 inches deep, chemical analysis has determined that the water originates from near Mesquite Flat.

Darwin Falls (topo: *Darwin*, elev: 3000, hike: 1¼ miles): This hike takes you along a year-round stream and to a 20 foot cascading waterfall. This trail is easier in winter, when the vegetation is not so intense in the canyon. The spring time is also good but walking will be slower as you weave around the plants along the stream. The trail may be muddy in some places, expect to get you boots wet. To find the falls turn south onto the Darwin Canyon Road, one mile west of Panamint Springs Resort. This dirt road will take you 2½ miles into the canyon. There is a small parking area at the trailhead.

Gower Gulch (topo: *Furnace Creek*, elev: 600, hike: 5.6 miles): Hike from Zabriskie Point through the Badlands to Golden Canyon. Within Gower Gulch you will have an opportunity to examine, close-up, the formations left by the receding prehistoric Lake Manly. You will encounter a couple of dry waterfalls that are easily descended as you approach Golden Canyon. This hike will provide you with some excellent opportunities to photograph the central part of the valley framed by the stark formations of the hills that form the sides of the gulch. The trail will lead you down into and through Golden Canyon.

Hole in Rock Spring (topo: *Chloride City*, elev: 3,000, hike: 1½ miles): This very short hike starts on the Daylight Pass Road 1¼ miles north of Hells Gate. Follow the trail that begins on the west side of the road and climbs over a low hill, and then turns north. On your way to the spring there are two sign posts with "Hole in Rock Spring" signs attached, neither of these signs is visible from the road. The trail will take you into a small canyon at the end of which you will find the spring in a very small cave. If you are considering attempting to crawl inside, be advised that this inviting place is also inviting to the many animals of the area. The floor of this small cave is always soggy and muddy. As you return to your vehicle, take a few minutes and walk down the wash that parallels the west side of the road. In about 200 yards you will be at the mouth of another very wide wash. On the north side of this, about 20 yards into the wash is the remnant of a small rock-walled hut. The age and purpose of this shelter is unknown.

Little Hebe Crater (topo: *Ubehebe Crater*, elev: 2,800, hike: 1 mile): Start at the parking lot of Ubehebe Crater. Follow the signs along the south rim. The trail is up-hill all the way, climbing 200 feet in elevation very quickly, and can be a formidable climb for the non-hiker. Keep in mind that the end is only ½ mile away, and the view is more than worth the effort. Take your camera. If you want a really good picture continue walking to the east side of Little Hebe, you will see it is in fact a crater, within a crater. Exploring the area will reveal two more small craters immediately to the west of Little Hebe. If you are inclined to investigate the terrain around Little Hebe, please be aware that treacherous drop-offs and very steep canyons are common in this area.

Red Wall and Fall Canyon (topo: *Fall Canyon, and Grapevine Peak*, elev: 1,600, hike: 14.5 miles): The best way to see these two most spectacular canyons is to hike north from the mouth of Titus Canyon along the upper edge of the fan for 3½ miles to Red Wall Canyon. This canyon is very colorful and narrow; moderate rock climbing skills are needed to

Little Hebe Crater

progress beyond the dry waterfall about 1 mile into the canyon. Starting very early in the day will permit a visit into beautiful Fall Canyon, with its extensive narrows, just ¾ of a mile north of Titus Canyon. A little over 2½ miles into the canyon is a 30 foot high dry waterfall, beyond which you will find outstanding examples of canyon narrows. The terrain in this area will make for a strenuous walk. Take your time, plenty of water, and a high energy lunch.

Telephone Canyon (topo: *Emigrant Canyon*, elev: 3,000, hike: 12.5 miles): Start 1½ miles up Emigrant Canyon Road from the junction at Highway 190. A faintly defined road crosses the wash here. Before proceeding, look closely for a road that climbs out of the wash on the east wall, slightly to the north of where you enter the wash. About 1½ miles from where you left the pavement you will enter a canyon with some fascinating red conglomerate rock formations and overhangs.

Follow the road for another mile to Telephone Canyon, identified by a wide canyon mouth which branches off toward the south. This canyon earned its name when it was used to route the telephone and telegraph lines from Rhyolite to Skidoo. About ¾ of a mile into the canyon you will find the remnants of an arastra, a structure designed for milling ore by using an animal to drag heavy stones around in an open shallow pit. A short way further into the canyon is a small, sandstone arch on the east wall above the canyon floor. Continuing on, following the remnants of an old road, will bring you over a hill and back out to Emigrant Canyon road about 2 miles south of your starting point.

Titus Canyon (topo: *Fall Canyon, and Thimble Peak*, elev: 960, hike: 6.5 miles): Even if you've driven through the canyon, this hike provides a whole new perspective. Titus Canyon exit road is open to two-way traffic and parking is available at the mouth of the canyon. You will experience first hand the grandeur of the narrows that entice visitors to make the 25 mile drive year after year. Be sure to hike up the canyon far enough to explore the area around Klare Spring. There are Petroglyphs, and Pictographs, on the rocks above the spring. In the interest of safety watch out for vehicles coming through the canyon.

Backpacking: With 5,189 square miles to hike in, you should not lack for a selection of terrain and scenery that suits you best. A hiker may choose to confine walking to the 200 square miles of salt pan that is 200 or more feet below sea level. Another might prefer to explore all of the 550 square miles that is at or below sea level. Others will head directly for the mountains and the high, cooler canyons where a mixture of history and geology keeps visitors coming back year after year for more. Rather than

Arch In Telephone Canyon

attempt to describe a series of hike locations in this limited space, the various portions of the Valley offering the best backpacking experiences will be discussed. With over 1,000 square miles of valley and five sets of mountains to explore, there is something here for hikers of every persuasion.

The Valley – Along the length and across the breadth of the great trough that forms the valley of Death Valley are salt pans, salt pinnacles, salt pools, waterfalls, sand dunes, alluvial fans, and all types of rock-strewn terrain from small gravel to boulders. Mesquite Flat just above the sand dunes, the Kit Fox Hills to the east of the dunes, and the foothills below Keane Wonder Mill on south to the Park Service residential area will provide excellent hiking experiences. The Salt Creek Hills in the central Valley, the Saratoga Springs area in the southern Park; Tule Spring, Gravel Well, and the other water sources along West Side Road provide a glimpse of the hydrology of Death Valley.

Grapevine Mountains – Some of the most beautiful canyons are to be found in this northeast range; Titus Canyon, Titanothere Canyon, Red Wall Canyon, Fall Canyon, and my absolute favorite, Phinney Canyon. Plan to spend several weeks at the minimum to explore these high places as most of the canyons have tremendous elevation gains, and many may be penetrated almost 10 miles.

Funeral Mountains – History abounds along the crest and in hidden canyons of this group. Keane Wonder Mill and Mine, Chloride City, Echo Canyon, Hole-in-the-Wall Canyon, Schwaub, Inyo Mine, Travertine Springs, and Indian Pass are but a few of the places to see.

Black Mountains – The home of Dante's View, the interior of the Black Mountains also plays host to the fabulous Greenwater Valley and site of Greenwater, Furnace, and Gold Valley. A dirt road takes off from Dante's View Road and continues almost 30 miles to the pavement between Salsberry and Jubilee Passes, with many more miles of dirt roads lacing this high plateau. Plan to spend some time in Coffin and Sheep Canyons, and do not neglect to take a hike from Gold Valley down through the Willow Spring area.

Cottonwood Mountains – These northwest mountains of the Panamint Range are probably the most heavily traveled by hikers and off-highway vehicles because of their ease of access, beautiful interior, and availability of water. Starting at the Racetrack Valley road-head near Ubehebe Crater in the north, a hiker may follow the dirt trail to Teakettle Junction, go east to and through Hidden Valley (a must during the spring flowering season!) to Goldbelt Springs, down through spectacular Marble Canyon, and circle back up Cottonwood Canyon to the trail in Hidden Valley. Cut across Ulida Flat to the southern end of the Racetrack to see the moving rocks, and then on out to your origin. This trek will require very tight planning in regards to routes and water supplies. Although many of the springs and streams here have been reasonably dependable, bring your own supply or cache it in advance. If you explore the area surrounding Tin Mountain, do it cautiously as there are many treacherous gorges, box canyons, and unstable rock walls.

Panamint Mountains – The Panamints are the highest of the mountains which hold Death Valley captive. There is a vast amount of history hidden in the canyons and on the plateaus of these mountains. Sites like Skidoo, Harrisburg, and Panamint City are honey combed with old mines and diggings, testimony to the dogged determination of the prospectors and miners that came to this area. The mountains also offer wonders like the

Hikers At Burned Wagons Point

79

Charcoal Kilns, Striped Butte, and Geologist's Cabin. You can almost forget that you are in the desert when you get into the pine forests on the upper slopes of these mountains.

The Big Trek – Walking the length of Death Valley without the benefit of experiencing some of the preceding treks could very well prove a waste of time. The difficulties and logistics involved in water caching for the Big Trek leaves a hiker little choice of route. My best recommendation is to obtain a copy of the hiker's guide, "Backpacking Death Valley," for a detailed discussion on the subject. There you will find ample space devoted to the planning, preparation, execution, and enjoyment of the Big Trek. If you have never had to use a sun shelter, cross the lower salt pan, or do split-day hiking, you might wish to investigate these things first. Regardless of your previous backpacking accomplishments or conquests, remember to walk slow, climb easy, and drink plenty of water.

Off Paved Highway Vehicle Trips

The Death Valley backcountry has more than enough roads through canyons, washes, and across mountain plateaus to keep a vehicle equipped for off-pavement travel busy for many years. Some of the roads will require the use of 4-wheel drive. The elevation gains, very narrow canyons with dry waterfalls, and deep gravel do demand better than average driving skills. The roads described here were selected for their historic and geologic significance.

NOTE: Driving off established dirt roads is strictly prohibited within the Park. All vehicles used on any roads within the park must be "street legal" and the drivers properly licensed. Although these roads may be clearly indicated on most maps, they are not intended for the family sedan. If you decide to travel by vehicle in the back country, follow the same precautions as for walking; tell someone where you are going and when you plan to return, and take plenty of water. Carry a tool kit that will permit minor repairs, as well as a jack and a good spare tire. Some of these trips will take you outside the boundaries of the Park. Here you may encounter private property or active mining claims, respect the rights of the property owners. One last thought, a line representing a road on a printed map does not relieve you of the responsibility for verifying, with the Park Service, that the road does in fact exist and that the area is open to vehicles.

Ballarat Loop – Using the Ballarat, Panamint, Manly Fall, and Manly Peak topo's, you will drive east out of Ballarat into Pleasant Canyon. This 28-mile trek will bring you along the ridge of the Panamints to view Butte Valley, the old talc mines in Warm Springs Canyon, and the southern portion of Death Valley. As you head south the plateaus of Middle Park and South Park Canyons are traversed. South Park Canyon is easily identified by the old dirt airstrip on its high wide plateau. From here you descend through the hairpin turns of this canyon back into Panamint Valley, just 3½ miles south of Ballarat. Be prepared for some significant side-hill driving while crossing the crest between the canyons, 4-wheel drive is required for this trip. For safety sake I recommend this trip for a group of at least three off highway equipped vehicles.

Echo Canyon/Chloride City Loop – This fantastic historical trek of nearly 100 miles in length will bring you over the Funeral Mountains twice. The loose gravel in Echo Canyon and sand in the Amargosa Desert will require 4-wheel drive. Start at Echo Canyon to see the Needles Eye, sites of Inyo Mine and Schwaub. The route can be deceptive. Proceeding up the canyon past the Inyo Mine site may seem like the thing to do, but the actual route is about ¾ of a mile back down the road. Follow this route to the northeast and drop down into the Amargosa Desert. Drive east, toward Big Dune, then turn north along the bed of the dismantled

Tonopah and Tidewater Railroad. Approximately 10 miles north of Big Dune, you turn southwest back toward the Funeral Mountains. You climb the eastern side of the Funerals to crest near the site of Chloride City. Cautiously work your way up and west to Chloride Cliffs and some breathtaking views of central Death Valley. There are two routes out of Chloride City; one will bring you to the park boundary on Nevada Highway 374, the other route puts you near Daylight Pass just north of Hell's Gate.

To plan this trip you need the Furnace Creek, Echo Canyon, Lee's Camp, Ashton, Carrara Canyon, East of Chloride City, and Chloride City topographic maps. Carry plenty of gas and water; a shovel and a hi-lift jack are great safety additions to your load.

Greenwater Exploratory – The immense interior between the Black Mountains and Greenwater Range is called Greenwater Valley. This area offers several days of interesting exploring, most of the trails can be traveled with any high clearance vehicle. A few side roads leading to the sites of Greenwater and Furnace are restricted to short wheel-base vehicles due to a series of narrow, deep gullies and high crests in the road. Don't miss beautiful Gold Valley at the southwestern edge of Greenwater Valley.

On the eastern side, you can hike the Greenwater Canyon trail 18 miles across the Greenwater Range to come out a few miles south of Death Valley Junction on State Route 127. This trail is closed to vehicles. It will take you out of the Park past the site of the Lila C Mine. An alternative would be to follow Greenwater Valley Road southeast and connect with Highway 178 near Salsberry Pass. This route will take you past the road to Gold Valley.

In order to explore all this area has to offer, I recommend the following topo's Greenwater Canyon, West of Eagle Mountain, Funeral Peak, Deadman Pass, and Salsberry Peak. Also expect a couple of spots of deep, soft sand traps on the road through Greenwater Valley.

Racetrack Valley Circuit – After enjoying the magnificence of Scotty's Castle and the depths of Ubehebe Crater, you are probably ready now to rough it a bit where the people are fewer and farther between. A usually well-graded road leaves from near the overlook at Ubehebe Crater and leads into Racetrack Valley. After a few rainstorms, the first 10 miles of

this road might give you more practice than you ever wanted in driving a deep, gravel covered road with high crown. Due to the proximity of the alluvial fans of Tin Mountain's west side, the Racetrack Valley Road has been known to be inundated with layers of gravel making progress slow and difficult.

Ten miles later, at Teakettle Junction, you may elect to make a left turn and pass through Hidden Valley, past Goldbelt Springs, over Hunter Mountain, and down into Saline Valley. Passing Teakettle Junction, staying to the right, drive to the south end of the Racetrack, a large, mud playa and hike ½ mile towards the extreme south end for sightings of the moving rocks. Do not drive onto the playa, it is closed to vehicles.

Southern Trek – A bit of history and a lot of scenery can be had traveling the southern roads of the Park. Portions of this trek are on well-graded roads, and some parts will vibrate your vitals. Start the historic adventure by driving onto West Side Road south of the exit from Artist's Drive. In a little over 5 miles you will pass the junction of Trail Canyon, a spectacular steep, rocky ride up the eastern side of the Panamints. Years ago, Trail Canyon was a favorite trip to Aguereberry Point for off-roaders. It has been closed as a through route due to major washouts and the Park Service has no plans to re-open it. At Shorty's Well, 4 miles to the south, Hanapauh Canyon offers another route into the Panamints, again with no outlet.

Driving 4 more miles down West Side Road will bring you to the Dayton-Harris graves. A monument erected by the Park Service and the Death Valley 49ers marks the site of the remains of Shorty Harris, famous prospector of Death Valley, and his friend, Jim Dayton manager of Greenland Ranch, now Furnace Creek Ranch. Just past the graves is the site of Eagle Borax Works, the first (but unsuccessful) borax operation in the Valley.

Further south are Bennett's Long Camp and Bennett's Well. Five miles south of Bennett's Long Camp is Johnson Canyon. Near the end of this canyon, a short hike from the end of the road, is the site of Hungry Bill's Ranch. Hungry Bill was the brother of Panamint Tom, a Shoshone Chief.

Another 12 miles south on the West Side Road brings you to the access road to Warm Springs Canyon. This canyon was the site of extensive talc mining operations until 1988. Ten miles into the canyon, the main road swings to the right and another road will be seen off to your left (a sign might still be there) which takes you into Butte Valley. This road may be rough riding for 6 miles or so until it breaks into the open valley. A high clearance vehicle, carefully driven, can take you south into Butte Valley to view the spectacular Striped Butte.

After returning from Butte Valley, continue south 3 miles to the end of West Side Road, turn right onto the pavement and stop to see the Ashford Mill ruins. Directly across the paved road (east) from the ruins is a dirt road leading up to the old Ashford Mine. Driving it will require 4-wheel drive, all the way. At the top, 3 miles later, the view of the southern Valley is excellent with sightings of Shoreline Butte, Cinder Hill, and even the old talc mines in Warm Springs Canyon.

Depending on recent weather conditions, you may want to consider another route out of Butte Valley. Shortly after passing the Butte is a road on your right leading up to what is called the "Geologist's Cabin," a well-built rock cabin commanding a fine view of the valley and the butte. This is a good area to take a break because of the scenery from the 4,000 foot plateau. Leaving the cabin, drive back down to the main road and head south through Mengel Pass, down through Goler Wash and Canyon. The

easy, but steep, narrow and winding, road down the wash will put you on the road to Ballarat, some 14 miles to the north. Be sure to stop in Ballarat to see the remains of the town.

Miscellaneous Treks: Though you may share the road with passenger cars, don't miss Titus Canyon. From wherever you stay in the Valley, begin your day early and head over Daylight Pass to near Rhyolite. Approximately two miles east of the Park boundary, turn west off Nevada Route 374 onto Leadfield Road (Titus Canyon trail-head), you must cross at least 10 miles of the Amargosa Desert before ascending Red Pass. Topping Red Pass is always an exciting experience as "Leadfield Canyon" stretches out below your feet. From here you begin the continuous descent through a series of canyons to end your trip at Titus Canyon.

About 4½ miles south of Hells Gate on the Beatty Cutoff Road is the road leading up to the Keane Wonder Mill site. This is another site that can be reached in a passenger car if one is careful. At the mill site, try to keep your children from climbing around the shaky structures or falling down the steep bank below the mill. The structures in the area are at least 90 years old and may not be safe for climbing in and exploring. Park you vehicle at the base of the hill, all the old trails in this area are closed to vehicles.

Three trails lead off from the bottom of the steep hill; one heads north and the other south; the third one leads up the hill to the mill site. The north route follows an old pipeline to Keane Springs which supplied the water for the mill operation, and much of the pipe is still in evidence on the right side of the trail. After a mile or so the trail might be overrun by foul-smelling water, depending on the recent weather. You should hike around this sulfurous mess to keep from being covered with mud smelling like rotten eggs that will hang on for quite awhile! Another half-mile and over a steep embankment will place you in front of a building that once served as the mine office and superintendent's quarters back in the early 1920s.

When you're back at the main trail leading to the mill, go up this trail for a short distance to another trail heading south into a small canyon. As you enter this canyon, you find a "two-holer" in very good shape tucked away in a crevice on your left (it's nice to know where these things are!). The trail increases in steepness and narrowness with shelves of rock layering an old road. Hiking another ¼ to ½ mile brings you to the narrows of the canyon and a strange wooden "bridge" spanning the walls at about head height. Many sightings of mine tunnels and cableways are found in this very short canyon.

There are three canyon trips in the southern portion Cottonwood Mountains; each provides varying terrain experiences as well as scenic satisfaction. The first is Lemoigne Canyon, which is a combination drive and hike. About 6 miles west of Stovepipe Wells Village on Highway 190 is the turnoff to Lemoigne Canyon. The 5 miles of road to the canyon head can usually be done with a high clearance vehicle. From this point the road has been closed by the Wilderness Act, the remainder of the trip must be undertaken on foot. In the main canyon, the walls begin to close in on you and a few small dry waterfalls are in evidence.

Near the end of the canyon the trail forks. The left fork heads up to Lemoigne's old silver-lead mine, and the right trail goes only another ½ mile past an old ore chute into a box canyon. Taking the left fork will bring you to an old tin-covered shack; this is presumed to have been Jean Lemoigne's home. In planning for this trip, you need the Stovepipe Wells, Cottonwood Canyon, and Panamint Butte topo's.

The trail out to Cottonwood and Marble Canyons leaves the north edge of the airstrip across the highway from Stovepipe Wells Village. The first

several miles would be a good place to have large floatation tires, but as the road ascends the fans of the Cottonwoods it turns to rock and gravel. After about 8 miles, the road drops off into a wash that is common to both canyons. The first sharp left turn, after a couple of miles, bring into view the Goldbelt Springs sign on a shelf to your right overlooking the road. Since this sign gets moved around a lot by pranksters, you must walk over to the shelf and look for the sometimes indistinct road heading westward. Once on the Marble Canyon road, you travel a minor wash for a mile and then enter the canyon. This road is only about 3½ miles long, and terminates where a huge boulder has wedged itself between the walls blocking the road. Park here, walk up to your right, and back down to the road to seek out some fine Petroglyphs and Pictographs.

The route to Cottonwood Creek through Cottonwood Canyon is a mixture of loose sand and gravel, with frequent sightings of pieces of dead cottonwood trees washed down from the stand around the springs. At the end of the road is a mass of Cottonwood trees with a bubbling creek passing through them. The scene is so totally out of place, that is difficult to believe it exists without seeing it. The road ends here, you cannot go all the way to Goldbelt Springs. Topo's needed for this trip are Stovepipe Wells, Cottonwood Canyon, and East of Sand Flat.

When the Valley temperatures are higher than comfortable an interesting ride to get away from it all is Phinney Canyon. The road starts off U.S. 95 about 11 miles north of Beatty on the way to Tonopah. The road is generally in good shape for the first 12 miles, but as the ascent of the eastern Grapevines begins, the next 8 miles will be pot luck. At about the 12 mile point, you see a trail branching to the right. You have just crossed the Sarcobatus Flat at an elevation of about 4,000 feet, and now the climb begins into Phinney Canyon. Unlike the Funeral and Black Mountains, the crest of the Grapevines is spotted with Pinyon and Limber pine. The trail gains almost 3,200 feet elevation in the next 7 miles, passes over the crest, and ends at 6,800 feet. The view from this altitude is without equal anywhere in the Valley. Having just passed between the two highest peaks in the Grapevine Mountains, Grapevine Peak at 8,738 feet and Wahguyhe Peak at 8,628 feet, there is little left to impede your view of Death Valley and the mountains beyond. You can see many springs in the immediate area, the most obvious being Doe Spring on your right as you pass the crest.

Backcountry Behavior

To some, the desert is looked upon as a coarse place; expansive, desolate, and lifeless. But the desert and especially Death Valley National Park is neither desolate nor lifeless. As you probably have seen, it is delicate and fragile. The impact to terrain and local vegetation from even a small amount of overuse or abuse proves the fragility of this desert basin.

The refuse left behind at once popular towns and camps is part of the history of the area. This kind of refuse is acceptable and "colorful." I'm referring to sardine cans, assorted wire, and other miscellaneous junk commonly found at the many mill and mine sites around the park. These items are fun, and at time educational, to look at when you realize their age goes back 70 to 100 or more years. It's the contemporary trash we wish to avoid – shiny, new beer cans, wine bottles, aluminum foil wrappers, and the like. If back country travelers had the space to carry them in full, they must certainly have enough space to take the empties back with them.

Of equal concern in this Park is the large amount of natural, and historic leave-alones – those items which the Park Service, and those of us that love the desert want to remain in their existing condition and position. A

much abused leave-alone is the "Driving Off Roads Prohibited" signs scattered throughout the Park. Abuses to delicate areas are not restricted to the actions of back country visitors as is evidenced by the missing headstone of Val Nolan, the exhumed graves at Skidoo, or the missing bronze plaque from Dante's View. As with all other National Parks, picking flowers, gathering firewood, collecting rocks, or removing artifacts is strictly prohibited.

When traveling the backcountry on foot or in a vehicle, you will notice many claim markers consisting of a pile of rocks or a large post set into the ground. Attached to the posts, and in or around the rocks, may be a tin can, bottle, or other container holding the old claim papers. It is probably an acceptable practice for the curious to remove the papers out of academic interest, but it is imperative that everything be returned as found. These are historic and sometimes private leave-alones of importance to those that put them there or people that may visit the area after us. Some of the claim markers identify current or active claims, and should not be altered or removed.

One last "leave-alone" is a water cache not belonging to you. These are a hiker's life-line, removing or damaging one could have catastrophic results for another back-country traveler. As the thirsty owner of a vandalized cache, I speak from experience of the empty, sinking feeling brought on by the realization that you must proceed very carefully lest you become a statistic. I would not want to even imagine that what I thought was a joke may have been the cause of another person's death.

Chapter 5
Well, Here We Are!

Planning

Death Valley is the largest national park in the 48 contiguous states. Its places of interest are widely scattered and separated by miles of roads. Even with this obstacle, there are ways which permit a visitor to the park to gain the maximum amount of enjoyment for the least expenditure of time and money.

Some folks are natural born planners; everything they do is tightly organized with little or no wasted time and effort. Others like to be more flexible in their approach and let things come as they may. There are also middle-of-the-road types who plan when the feeling strikes them, but let everything "hangloose" when so inclined. Whichever category best describes your traveling mode, I hope to convince you that a planned trip to Death Valley will save you time, money, and frustration.

Death Valley Gateway

To simplify matters, you should consider four key elements before taking a trip to the park. After all, there is nothing more discouraging than arriving at a place as large and as intricate as Death Valley, finding yourself in some obscure location, and looking around and saying "Well, here we are!"

Death Valley National Park does have a modest visitor fee. As of this printing the fee is $5.00 for a seven day stay. This fee is collected either at the Visitor Center or at the Grapevine Ranger Station on the way to Scotty's Castle. Keep your receipt to demonstrate proof of payment.

First

How long will you be in the park? If you are driving through with little or no time for side trips, your route should take you past Furnace Creek. Here you should at least spend an hour of your time visiting the two museums; the Borax Museum behind Furnace Creek Ranch, and the Death Valley Museum in the Park Service Visitor Center. Both of the museums are free and give you a preview of what you can expect to see if you return with more time available.

Visiting the Valley for a weekend with one overnight will require tight planning. Since a major portion of the historical and geological points of interest are centered around Furnace Creek, you should plan to stay there. If you have not planned to spend much time in the Furnace Creek area, do not miss the museums. However, staying at Furnace Creek overnight will allow you to see a dozen or more points of interest all within 10 miles driving distance.

Over a 3-day weekend, you will spend a considerable amount of time driving to see the key attractions of the park. Look carefully at the Death Valley maps, read the next three chapters, and organize your time so that you will be at the right place at the right time.

With a week or more of vacation time, you should be able to visit almost every major point of interest. You can enter the park at the north or south end and work your way to the opposite end. Due to the heavy concentration of things to see and do at Furnace Creek, plan to spend a significant amount of time in its vicinity.

Second

When do you expect to visit the park? The extreme weather conditions in Death Valley make it necessary to be selective about the time of year you choose for your visit. Summer trips into the Valley proper are not normally recommended, and there is very little to see comfortably at that time. However, in summer there are many sights to see in the Panamints as well as the eastern mountains, and the weather can be quite pleasant at the higher elevations.

The facilities at Stovepipe Wells Village, Scotty's Castle, Panamint Springs Resort, and Furnace Creek Ranch as well as the main park roads are normally open the entire year. Keep in mind that the wettest months are November and January. This doesn't mean that you will risk a soaking going across the salt flats, but it does mean that some of the popular canyons and other side trips might be closed due to washouts.

Death Valley Museum & Visitor Center

The "ideal time" to visit Death Valley is a matter of personal opinion; October and November are generally comfortable with possible showers around mid-November. December through February are likely to be considerably cooler and wetter. March and April are usually windswept with dust and sand storms, in the general area of the sand dunes, lasting from 6 hours to 4 days. Since this is also the flower season, these months are well worth a the minor discomfort of the wind and sand.

There are several periods during the year you can expect the Valley to be filled to capacity. In November for the Death Valley 49ers Encampment during the second weekend, Thanksgiving Week, Christmas until the New Year, Presidents Day Weekend, and the Spring Break weeks before and after Easter Sunday. Every year the heaviest park visitation is during the Spring Break school holiday period

At these peak periods upwards of 50,000 visitors may partake of the Valley's sites and scenes. You might have to wait 4 hours to get into Scotty's Castle, or line up for over an hour at any of the three gas stations. Restaurants are also at capacity, so bring a snack to eat while you wait in line to have dinner. Even the backcountry trails are unusually populated during these times. At least you won't have to wait long to be rescued should you become stranded in a remote location. If your visit to Death Valley is less than a week, plan to come in between these holiday periods for a better introduction to the Valley unencumbered by the numbers of people.

Despite the crowds and the attendant discomfort of waiting to eat, get gas, or see a sight, visitors should not miss the opportunity to enjoy the 49ers Encampment the second weekend in November. During these four exciting days (Thursday through Sunday), the Death Valley 49ers' program offers an outdoor art exhibit at the Visitor Center, special breakfasts to introduce authors, photographers, and artists, and specially guided tours and talks of the Valley. The evenings are filled with patio dances, a fiddler's contest, and numerous campfire programs with professional entertainment. Every hour of every day has an event; a burro-flapjack race, gunfights, wagon trains, trail rides, music, and special hiking groups.

Third
What kind of accommodations will you use? Whether your plans are to vehicle camp, tent camp, or select a motel or inn, there is a place for you in Death Valley. The National Park Service operates 8 campgrounds at widespread locations throughout the Valley. In addition, three settlements, Furnace Creek Ranch, Panamint Springs Resort, and Stovepipe

Wells Village offer limited private camping facilities. Park Service campground information is as follows:

Furnace Creek Campground: This is a pleasant campground on the west side of the Visitor Center with some shaded sites. The entry road is ¼ mile north of the Death Valley Visitor Center. This is usually the first area to fill up during holiday periods and on most weekends during the season; individual sites have tables and fire places. Fresh water, and flush toilets are available and conveniently located; water is not available at the individual sites. There is a tank disposal station.

Mahogany Flat Campground: This is the highest campground or area that can be driven to in Death Valley at 8,200 feet. The grade to these 8 sites is steep and often very rough, and not recommended for passenger cars or vehicles with trailers. This campground has pit toilets, tables, and fireplaces. There is no water, and it is closed in the winter. This campground was named for the Desert Mahogany, a shrub or small tree that is native to desert regions.

Mesquite Springs Campground: A beautifully placed campground at an elevation of 1,800 feet, this campground is located about 5 miles south of Mesquite Junction near the Grapevine Ranger Station. The sites are built on a large shelf overlooking Death Valley Wash with good views of Tin Mountain and the immense network of alluvial fans originating from the Cottonwood Mountains. Shade is not available at the sites, and the eastern edge of the campground is ringed with mesquite trees. The mesquite is armed with long thorns, so watch the children. Sightings of Coyote, Kit Fox, and Owls are not uncommon. Tables, fire places, fresh water, flush toilets, and a tank disposal station are available.

Stovepipe Wells Campground: A large, level, and open area, this campground is situated opposite Stovepipe Wells Village just three miles west of the sand dunes. Those in tents should set up along the outer edges away from vehicular dust. In the event of a sand storm, very likely in March and April, maintain as low a profile as possible near the mesquite and creosote bush rimmed perimeter. Fresh water (not to sites) and flush toilets are available. A tank disposal station is situated near the restrooms. Watch your children on the entry road as this is also the entrance to the airstrip and a popular back-country road.

Sunset Campground: This is the largest camping area available in the Park with over 1,000 sites designed primarily for recreation vehicle camping. The campground entrance is about one-tenth of a mile south of Furnace Creek Ranch. The level, open area is across the highway from the Ranch and Date Palm orchard, and it has easy access to both the Visitor Center or Ranch facilities. A tank disposal station is located near the highway at the north end of this campground. Both flush and pit toilets, and water are available, but there is no water or other hook-ups to the individual sites. Sunset campground is closed during the summer months.

Texas Spring Campground: Nestled in the small hills above Furnace Creek Inn and overlooking the Furnace Creek area are two levels of sites, some with shade provided by Tamarisk trees. Fireplaces, tables, flush and pit toilets are available. Texas Spring is reached by the same access road as Sunset. A tank disposal station is located on the entrance road to the first level. Tent campers should obtain sites as close to the hills as practical due to gusty winds. A portion of the sites are limited to tent campers only. If your children love to climb around hills, check the area first yourself for drop-offs before you let them run free. This campground is usually closed after Easter Week.

Thorndike Campground: Situated ½ mile past the Charcoal Kilns in Wildrose Canyon, this 10-site campground at 7,500 feet is well shaded just where you need it least. The position of the campground in relation to the mountains makes for a very short day of sunlight; you can expect the sun to disappear below the horizon at about 3:00pm Early one October, I left the very hot Valley to cool off and get some photographs of Skidoo, so I decided to camp at Thorndike. After nearly freezing, I left first thing the next morning. The entry road to these sites is not recommended for trailers and sometimes passenger cars will have a bad time as well. Like Mahogany Flat, this area is closed in the winter. The last time I was there it offered pit toilets, fireplaces, tables, and water. Thorndike Campground is named for a miner that dreamed of building a hotel atop Telescope Peak.

Wildrose Campground: This small campground has about 12 sites. It is located 40 miles north of Trona and 5 miles from the south-western Park boundary on the road to Wildrose Canyon and the Charcoal Kilns. At 4,100 feet elevation, it can get a little chilly in mid-season. This is an excellent camp for those who wish to explore Aguereberry Point, Harrisburg, Skidoo, and other western Panamint sights. Facilities include pit toilets, water, some tables, and fire places. There is no gasoline available close by. The campground is open all year and is near the Wildrose Ranger Station. Just as a cautionary note, I have seen snow in Wildrose Canyon as early as mid-November.

Most of the established campgrounds within the Park are fee areas, and as of this writing, the fees were:

Campground	Fee / Day	Season
Furnace Creek	$10.00	Year Round
Mahogany Flat	Free	Mar.-Nov.
Mesquite Spring	$6.00	Year Round
Stovepipe Wells	$6.00	Oct.-Apr.
Sunset	$6.00	Oct.-Apr.
Thorndike	Free	Mar.-Nov.
Texas Spring	$6.00	Oct.-Apr.
Wildrose	Free	Year Round

For exact information on the various camping areas and their fees, check with the Park Service or obtain a camping brochure. Each campground has a stay limit. This is usually 14 days, but in early 1995 campers were permitted to stay in Texas Spring Campground for up to 30 days. Camping reservations, for Furnace Creek only, may be made through HSN MISTIX Corporation at 1-800-365-2267 (TDD 1-800-274-7275), reservations can be made up to eight weeks in advance.

For the "indoor" camper, there are three locations providing the basics of comfortable living and good eating. If accommodations are full in the valley, Appendix A includes a listing of motels with their addresses and telephone numbers in surrounding towns.

Furnace Creek Inn: Considered a luxury accommodation, the Inn is located against a hillside overlooking central Death Valley and Furnace Creek Ranch. The Inn is open from early October to the end of May with 67 units on the American plan (meals included). Guest services like a beauty shop, barber, swimming pools, dining room, and cocktail lounge are available within the Inn. The Inn was built by the Pacific Coast Borax Company in 1926. In the late 1950s, the Inn was operated for the borax company by Fred Harvey, Inc., which in turn bought the Ranch and Inn

Entrance To Furnace Creek Ranch

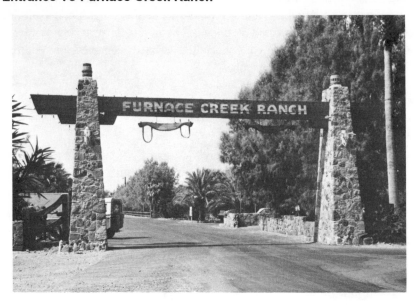

properties around 1966. You will notice a stone monument topped by a large cross at the north end, and below, the Inn. This marker honors Steve Esteves, head stone mason for the Pacific Coast Borax Company, who was responsible for the beautiful stone work around the Inn and the Ranch.

Furnace Creek Ranch: The Ranch offers a wide range of simple cabins, pool-side rooms, golf-side rooms, and deluxe motel units. A few vehicle camping sites with hookups are also available. There are many services available at the ranch, such as a golf course, swimming pool, Borax Museum, guided bus tours of the valley, a coffee shop, restaurant, cocktail lounge, general store, guided horse-back rides, post office and an airstrip. Propane and diesel fuel may be purchased at the Furnace Creek service station, which also provides minor auto repairs. Charcoal and presto logs are also available at the general store. A recent addition is a frozen yogurt shop immediately behind the reservation office. Ice may be purchased in blocks or cubes from a machine just north of the service station.

Furnace Creek Ranch was first loosely settled by "Bellerin" Teck Bennett to grow alfalfa, barley and quail to feed the miner's and their animals in the early 1880s. The Ranch was taken over by W. T. Coleman's borax company to provide feed for their mules and a repair station for the wagons. In 1907, the Greenland Ranch became Furnace Creek Ranch and was expanded to meet the needs of the borax company due to its increased mining endeavors at nearby Ryan.

For further information call or write:

Furnace Creek Ranch	Furnace Creek Inn
P.O. Box 1	P.O. Box 1
Death Valley, CA 92328	Death Valley, CA 92328
(619) 786-2345	(619) 786-2361

Panamint Springs Resort: This small resort is tucked in the southwest corner of the new section of the Park. It is on the western edge of Panamint Valley along Highway 190. The resort offers a small motel, a coffee shop, gasoline, propane, a private campground with and without full hook-ups for RV's, showers, and an airstrip. They are planning to add a swimming pool in the near future. They are open all year.

For information you can call or write:

Panamint Springs Resort
P. O. Box 395
Ridgecrest, CA 93556
619-764-2010

Stovepipe Wells Village: This is a nostalgic place. The hotel offers small patio rooms, motel units, and deluxe rooms. A general store, gas station, swimming pool, restaurant, showers, cocktail lounge, gift shop, and small airstrip are also available. The hotel is open from October to May, and you may call to ask about trailer hookups or motel availability. As of this writing, the gas station and general store are open year round.

For information call or write:

October thru May	May thru October
Stovepipe Wells Village	Furnace Creek Ranch
Death Valley, CA 92328	P.O. Box 1
619-786-2387	Death Valley, CA 92328
	619-786-2345

The original Stovepipe Wells Hotel was opened for business in November 1926 by Helene and Bob Eichbaum, and was called "Bungalow City."

Stovepipe Wells Village

One of the first roads into the northern part of the valley was the Death Valley Toll Road over Townes Pass. This road officially opened earlier in the same year as the village. The charge for automobiles was $2 plus 50 cents for each passenger. In 1934, two years after Bob Eichbaum's death, the California Division of Highways bought the rights to the toll road from Helene Eichbaum. The Village is now owned by the National Park Service and operated by Amfac Hotels and Resorts (via Fred Harvey, Inc.). The colorfully constructed and decorated interiors of the buildings display artifacts of the mining days, and indicate the concern of the Park Service for maintaining Stovepipe Wells Village as a historic site.

Fourth

How will you get to the Valley? Since the vast majority of visitors drive, you might be well advised to decide which one of a variety of routes is best for you and your vehicle. The roads into the valley can be described as better than average, considering the environment and the cost reduction trends of many county maintenance budgets. The paved roads within the park are excellent.

The main route through the Park is California State Highway 190. This highway connects U.S. 395 on the west at Olancha, to California 127 in the east at Death Valley Junction. Approaching the valley from the west on this highway puts Townes Pass (elev. 4956ft) on your route. This steep pass climbs approximately 3,800 feet in less than 8 miles. The grade will tax the capabilities of many vehicles towing trailers and motorhomes. Radiator water tanks are placed at regular intervals on both sides of the pass. I recommend that you don't use your vehicle's air conditioner when climbing this pass.

If you are coming to the Park from Southern California, you can save considerable time and mileage by connecting with Highway 190 via Highway 178 through Trona. Although the road is not a nice as the sometimes four lane U.S. 395, its only drawback is that it is two lanes the whole way, but it also has a lot less traffic. Follow the signs for Ridgecrest and then Trona after leaving U.S. 395. North of Trona, in the Panamint Valley, the highway will fork. Take the left fork. This is Panamint Valley Road. You may be tempted to take Wildrose-Trona Road (the right fork) but this road is mostly dirt from just inside the Park boundary to Wildrose Canyon. From Wildrose to the Valley this winding road also has some very tight turns and is not recommended for large vehicles (longer than 25 feet) or any vehicles towing trailers.

Most visitors from California will find that their best approach to the park is one that will have them approaching from the south. During the prime visitor season, other available routes may have delays due to snow on the mountain passes.

An alternative for California visitors would be to bypass U.S. 395 and take Highway 58 or Interstate 15 to Baker. From Baker take Highway 127 north to Death Valley Junction and turn east on Highway 190. This route has gradual climbs and the road is in very good shape, although it is only two lanes. This is my preferred route whenever I tow a travel trailer or drive a motorhome to the valley. It's easier on the vehicle and, more importantly, easier on my nerves.

From the Pacific Northwest visitors usually follow U.S. 395 to Reno and continue south on that route. These visitors can connect with Highway 190 via Highway 136, just south of Lone Pine. An alternative for drivers

Remains of Rhyolite to Skidoo Telephone Line

coming south from Reno is U.S. 95 to Beatty, and then Nevada Route 374 west. This route does take you over Daylight Pass (elev. 4317ft), but the climb is much shorter than Townes Pass, about 900 feet in just under 7 miles. Some people coming from the north may decide to leave U.S. 95 at Scotty's Junction and enter the valley via Scotty's Castle. Most maps show this to be a direct straight route, but actually the road from the castle to Highway 190 snakes its way along the fans of the Grapevine Mountains all the way down Mesquite Flat.

Coming from Las Vegas is easy, head west on U.S. 95. As you approach the valley you have two options. One is to turn south on Nevada Route 373 at Amargosa Valley, this will change to California 127 when you cross the state line. You will then turn west on Highway 190 at Death Valley Junction. This is actually the shortest route to Furnace Creek from Las Vegas, and does not have any mountain passes. The second is to continue on U.S. 95 to Beatty and then follow Route 374 to the valley.

Other Services

To the east of the valley, 41 miles from Furnace Creek, Beatty, Nevada offers a wide variety of automobile and other services, for example, tire sales and repairs, welding, and mechanical or body repairs. For the do-it-yourselfer there is an auto parts retailer. You will also find a Bank of America branch complete with Automated Teller Machine. In addition to these, Beatty offers a variety of restaurants, casinos, and motels. For more extensive services, Las Vegas is 100 miles east of Beatty.

To the southwest of the park, 94 miles from Furnace Creek, Trona offers services similar to those of Beatty. Trona is a smaller town and hence the choices are more limited. As an alternative, Ridgecrest, a fair sized town, is only 29 miles south of Trona. Ridgecrest is the closest town for services like a hospital, major pharmacy, grocery stores, and new-car dealer repair shops.

Rental Cars are not available in the valley, the nearest agency is in Las Vegas. You will also find commercial airlines at Las Vegas.

The nearest hospital services are in Las Vegas, Lone Pine, and Ridgecrest. Beatty offers limited medical assistance through a Physicians Assistant, a licensed medical practitioner, linked directly to a complete staff of doctors in Las Vegas.

Emergency care within the Park is limited to first-aid provided by rescue personnel, thus it is based on the demands of any given situation. In the event of an emergency call 911 or 619-786-2330 for assistance 24 hours a day.

An Inyo County Sheriff is permanently stationed at Furnace Creek Ranch. Directions to the office can be obtained at either the Visitor's Center or the Furnace Creek Registration Office. Also during the periods of heavy visitor populations the California Highway Patrol does assist in patrolling the major roads.

Park Service

As with all the parks I have visited in our National Park System, the staff at Death Valley is very knowledgeable and friendly. They will provide you with up-to-date information on road conditions and travel status, weather reports, and camp grounds. From time to time the Park Service staff may close an area or restrict an activity. Keep in mind this is either for your safety or the preservation of this very delicate environment.

This is not a personal issue. It is a small part of their responsibility to protect visitors as well as the park.

A nice thing about the Park Service is that you can always find them when you need them. There are Ranger Stations throughout the park, and all are open from 8:00am until at least 4:00pm daily. Ranger Stations are located at Furnace Creek Visitor Center, Stovepipe Wells Village, Grapevine Ranger Station (near Mesquite Springs Campground), Scotty's Castle, Beatty, Shoshone, and Wildrose Canyon. The Rangers also regularly patrol the major roads within the Park.

If you need specific information regarding your visit or some aspect of the park, you can call or write the Park Headquarters. Their telephone number is 619-786-2331. The address is Death Valley National Park, Death Valley, CA 92328.

What To Do

The next three chapters are devoted entirely to the sites, history, geology, and wonders of Death Valley National Park. Each chapter is dedicated to a specific geographic area of the park.

Within each chapter, I have provided a reference map of the area being discussed. Each map contains all the normally open roads, as well as the locations of all the sites discussed in that chapter. The reference maps are presented on two facing pages. They are arranged with the western portion on the left, and the eastern area on the right page.

Within each chapter the sites are listed alphabetically. A map reference is included which corresponds to a grid that has been overlaid on the map near the beginning of the chapter. For each site I have attempted to include information relative to its history, importance, or visual significance. Some of the sites hold a special attraction for me and I have attempted to share that feeling with the reader.

In addition to these chapters, I have included a road mileage matrix in Appendix B. Finding the intersection of the appropriate column and row for two sites will provide the total mileage between them. Lastly for those, like me, who simply cannot live without an index, a comprehensive one is provided.

Chapter 6
North Park

Area

This chapter discusses the northern portion of the park. I use an imaginary line connecting Chloride Cliffs, the Sand Dunes, and Salt Lake to separate this section from the rest of the park. The north area includes Eureka Valley, Mesquite Flat, the Nevada Triangle and Saline Valley. The elevations in this area range from Sea Level to 8,900 feet. The environment here offers more vegetation, because this area receives a higher average rainfall and has generally lower average temperatures than the other sections of the park.

From east to west, the mountains you will find in this area are the Bullfrog Hills, in the Nevada Triangle; the Grapevine Mountains and Cottonwood Mountains, outlining Death Valley; the Last Chance Range and Inyo Mountains, defining Eureka Valley; and the Saline Range and Nelson Range, bordering Saline Valley. In addition to these mountains, there are three sets of sand dunes, the Eureka Dunes, some minor dunes on the west side of Eureka Valley, and the dunes near Salt Lake. The Death Valley Dunes are near Stovepipe Well, at the southern limit of this area, and are described in Chapter 7, Center Park.

This area abounds with natural and man-made phenomena. These include one of the steepest tramways in the United States, a castle, volcanic craters, un-explained moving rocks, and the largest sand dunes in North America. The plant life in this area is considered abundant for a desert, which is in direct contrast to that of the central and southern portions of the park. Two examples of this are Creosote Bush Desert and the Lee Flat Joshua Tree Forest.

An 1891 U.S. Geologic Survey map names the northern portion of Death Valley, above the Sand Dunes, as Lost Valley. This same map also includes what we today call Eureka Valley as Termination Valley.

Favorite Places

Some of my most favorite places are found at this end of the park. I am always drawn to Ubehebe Crater. The stark contrasts of the volcanic ash

Death Valley - North

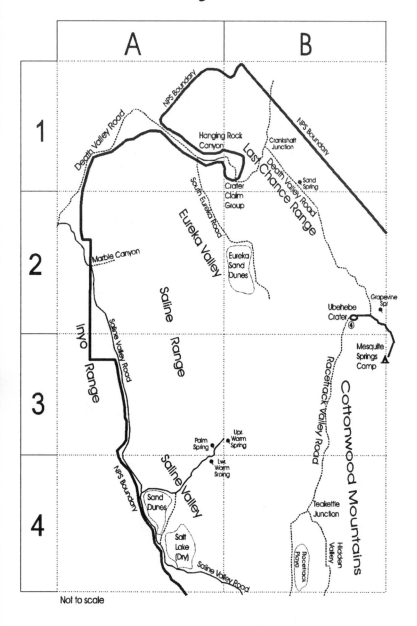

A

B

1

NPS Boundary

Death Valley Road

Hanging Rock
Canyon

Crankshaft
Junction

Last Chance Range

NPS Boundary

Death Valley Road

Sand
Spring

Crater
Claim
Group

South Eureka Road

Eureka Valley

2

Marble Canyon

Eureka
Sand
Dunes

Saline Range

Grapevine
Spr.

Ubehebe
Crater

Mesquite
Springs
Camp

Inyo Range

Saline Valley Road

3

Racetrack Valley Road

Cottonwood Mountains

Palm
Spring

Upr.
Warm
Spring

Lwr.
Warm
Spring

Saline Valley

4

NPS Boundary

Sand
Dunes

Teakettle
Junction

Salt
Lake
(Dry)

Racetrack
Playa

Hidden
Valley

Saline Valley Road

Not to scale

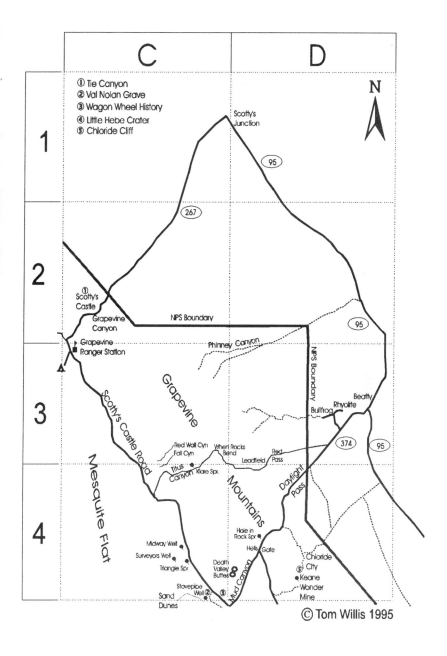

C

D

N

① Tie Canyon
② Val Nolan Grave
③ Wagon Wheel History
④ Little Hebe Crater
⑤ Chloride Cliff

1

Scotty's
Junction

95

267

2

①
Scotty's
Castle

Grapevine
Canyon

NPS Boundary

95

Grapevine
Ranger Station

Phinney Canyon

NPS Boundary

Grapevine

3

Beatty

Rhyolite

Bullfrog

Scotty's Castle Road

Red Wall Cyn
Fall Cyn

Wheri Rocks
Bend

Red
Pass

374

95

Titus
Canyon

Klare Spr.

Leadfield

Mesquite Flat

Mountains

Daylight Pass

4

Hole in
Rock Spr.

Midway Well

Hells Gate

Chloride

Surveyors Well

⑤ City

Triangle Spr.

Death
Valley
Buttes

Keane
Wonder
Mine

Stovepipe
Well ②

③

Mud Canyon

Sand
Dunes

© Tom Willis 1995

107

and the colors revealed in the rock strata are continually changing, not only from year to year but from hour to hour as the sun moves across the sky.

I always like to check out Scotty's Castle to stay abreast of the what the Park Service is doing. Their living history approach to presenting this home to visitors, is great. You almost expect Scotty or Mr. Johnson to greet you at the door. I also appreciate seeing their efforts at preserving this historic site for future generations of visitors.

Racetrack Valley is like a magnet for me. I am simply fascinated with the moving rocks. The thought of a rock as big as a 19-inch television moving on its own, is the ultimate brain teaser. Yes, there are actually rocks with trails "behind" them.

I also like to drive through Titus Canyon time after time. I usually do this at least once per season. I like to spend my time here out of my truck investigating the many side canyons and washes.

To See and Do
Big Pine / Death Valley Road (A1, B1, B2)
This road joins Ubehebe Crater Road 2.9 miles west of the junction at Grapevine Ranger Station. There are no services on this road. The nearest gasoline is at Scotty's Castle or Big Pine. The surface of the road is dirt for 42 of its 68 miles. The first 12 or so miles of the road is usually wash-board bumpy, but it tends to get smoother the further you drive away from the paved road. You will reach the Sand Spring area 9.1 miles from the paved road, where there are a number of small springs around the primary spring.

The next major feature along the road is Crankshaft Junction. There is a home-made directional sign here which appropriately includes a crankshaft and various other engine parts. At this junction you want to turn so that you will be heading roughly southwest (the left fork). From the junction the road climbs through the Last Chance Range.

At the summit of the Last Chance Range is the Crater Claim Group. The elevation here is approximately 5,200 feet. This active mining area is just outside the park boundary, as is the remainder of the road to Big Pine.

This area was excluded from the park to permit the operation of the mine and to allow commercial traffic to use the road. Your route will take you down the east side of the mountain range through Hanging Rock Canyon. The road is paved through the canyon, but the pavement will continue only for the length of the canyon.

Two miles east of Hanging Rock Canyon is the junction with Eureka Valley Road and the route to Eureka Sand Dunes. Pavement begins again 8.2 miles east of this junction. After 9 miles on the pavement you will come to a forest of Joshua Trees, another 2.3 more miles and you will enter the Inyo National Forest and begin the drive over the Inyo Mountains.

The intersection with Saline Valley Road is 3.2 miles east of the national forest boundary. This road is discussed later in this chapter. Big Pine / Death Valley Road ends at California Highway 168, about 5 miles north of Big Pine.

Chloride City (D4)
This is the site of a ghost town in the Funeral Mountains high above Keane Wonder Mine. This town actually boomed twice, once in 1871 and again in 1909. Both times the silver veins ran out and so did the life of the town.

Mine Site At Chloride City

Today, a visit to the site of Chloride City will provide you with an opportunity to investigate close up the "Cousin Jack" type houses, a style brought to the area by Irish and Welsh miners. There are also remnants of the mining efforts in the area like old stationary engines, water tanks, and various pipelines. Be careful when driving in the area, the hills are honey-combed with mines; some of these are immediately under the very roads you may attempt to drive on.

The town site can be reached by two routes. The first begins in Boundary Canyon on the way to Daylight Pass. The turnoff for this 4-wheel drive route is 3.3 miles north of Hells Gate, this road goes for 4.5 miles to the town. A couple of sections of this road does require 4-wheel drive.

The second route can be traveled by a high clearance vehicle; this route begins on the south side of Nevada Highway 374 immediately opposite the sign marking the park boundary. Take this road 7 miles south, then turn west for another 4.5 miles.

Chloride Cliffs (D4)
These cliffs are almost directly above Keane Wonder Mine. The cliffs are reached by taking a 4-wheel drive route for 2 miles south from Chloride City. The view of central Death Valley is spectacular from this overlook. I particularly like the morning light for taking pictures of the valley from here.

Along the road to the cliffs be on the look-out for an unusual one-stamp ore mill. This is so unique that it needs close-up inspection to actually determine what it is. This mill may have been the one that was used by Irving Crowell when he worked a mine near here from 1909 until 1917.

Death Valley Buttes (D4)
Dedicated and determined hikers will find a trip up either of these small mountains a challenge. I recommend that if you intend to make this climb, start your assault from the north face about a mile from Hells Gate. The climb on this side is less steep.

When you reach the summit of the first butte you can then walk along the narrow crest to the peak of the southern butte. This higher peak is called Red Top with an elevation of 3017 feet. The view of Mesquite Flat and the Sand Dunes are great. Be sure to take your camera, and water.

Death Valley Wash (B2, B3, C3)
This huge wash runs generally NNW to SSE for nearly 40 miles, beginning near Sand Spring and ending at a point about 8 miles north of Titus Canyon exit road. This wash parallels and is just to the west of Big Pine Road and the highway to Scotty's Castle. It forms a kind of natural hiker's trail and in some places is more like a canyon than a wash. Just west of Mesquite Springs Campground the walls of the wash are nearly ten feet tall. Walking this wash for any significant distance will require water caching along the way.

Eureka Sand Dunes (B2)
These dunes were closed to vehicles approximately 20 years before being included in Death Valley National Park. They were designated as a National Natural Landmark by the Bureau of Land Management to protect them for future generations. The main dunes tower 700 feet over the valley floor and are reputed to be the largest dunes in North America. The dunes are created by sand laden winds coming from the north meeting with opposing winds coming off the mountains to the east and south.

These dunes are home to two endemic plants, Eureka Dune Grass and Eureka Dunes Evening Primrose. The plants have been designated as endangered species. The dunes hold enough water to sustain these plants

The Eureka Dunes

and the others that grow on the sand, damp sand can usually be found by digging just a few inches with your fingers. There are also four endemic species beetles found on the dunes. Be careful not to step on the fragile plants or crush animal burrows as you explore the dunes.

These dunes are known as "singing" dunes. When the wind is blowing there is humming sound produced by the grains of sand rubbing together. Some say it sounds like an airplane flying in the distance.

The Eureka Sand Dunes can be reached by taking Big Pine Road north from near Ubehebe Crater. This wide dirt road will require a high-clearance vehicle. The turn off onto South Eureka Valley Road is 33½ miles from Ubehebe Crater Road, the dunes are another 10 miles south of this turn off. Be careful not to get stuck in loose sand as you approach the dunes. The dunes can easily be reached with a high clearance 2-wheel drive vehicle. Camping is permitted at the dunes, but no water is available at the dunes.

There are two alternatives to the route mentioned above. One is Death Valley Road, from Highway 168 near the town of Big Pine. The second is Saline Valley Road going up the west boundary of the park from Highway 190. (See the description of Saline Valley Road, later in this chapter.)

Eureka Valley Dunes (A2)
These minor sand dunes are at the base of the Saline Range on the west side of Eureka Valley. They appear to have been created by the same sand laden winds that created the Eureka Dunes. These dunes can be seen by looking west from almost any point in southern Eureka Valley. There is no vehicle access road to these dunes, but they can be reached by hiking about 3 miles west from South Eureka Valley Road, start your walk 2½ miles north of the Eureka Dunes.

Fall Canyon (C3)
This exceptional canyon is ¾ mile north of Titus Canyon. It can be reached by walking along the top of the fan, starting from the parking lot outside the mouth of Titus Canyon. This canyon is much narrower than Titus Canyon and the walls appear to be at least as high. Hiking into the canyon you will find the first dry waterfall after about a ½ mile, another one is just about at the 1 mile point. The narrow canyon continues for another 3½ miles.

Grapevine Canyon (C2)

This is a colorful canyon cutting through the northern Grapevine Mountains. Scotty's Castle is in the center of this canyon. On the way to the castle, take a moment to look at the unusual erosion of the sides of the canyon. There is a profusion of small holes in hillsides, some of which may be homes to the bats that live in the area. Wild grapes are known to have grown in this canyon and were the source of the name for the canyon and surrounding mountains.

Grapevine Springs (B2)

These springs, just north of Ubehebe Crater Road and east of Big Pine / Death Valley Road, are the water source for Scotty's Castle. The area around the springs is fenced and closed to the public. Inside this fenced area is a fine, small house said to have been built for Death Valley Scotty by Albert Johnson. I'm not sure how much time Scotty spent here; all the stories about him focus on his time at the castle and his antics around the country.

The area around the springs was at one time home to the largest and most prosperous Shoshone village in Death Valley; it's not clear if the village or the people were called "Mahunu." In the mid-1800s about 30 Shoshone people lived in the area.

Puffball - The Prospector's Medicine

Hells Gate (D4)

This site, at the junction of Daylight Pass Road and the Beatty Cut-off Road is appropriately named. As you approach the valley from the north-east, this is the first point that offers a view of what lies ahead. Imagine being here in July, on foot, with a burro for a companion. One story has it that this is the point when the drivers of freight wagons between Rhyolite and Skidoo would get the first blast of heat rising from the valley.

On one spring morning I found this very strange plant, a "Puffball," growing just off the road here. It is said that the miners used this plant as a healing agent for cuts and abrasions. The proper name for this plant is *Tulostoma simulans*.

Be sure to stop at the kiosk, just off the road, and check out the view of the southern and central valley. During the flower season the area between Hells Gate and Mud Canyon is covered with flowers of every size and color. Photographing the valley from this vantage point is best in early to mid morning.

Hidden Valley (B4)

This area is a 7 mile ride from Teakettle Junction and 25 miles south of Ubehebe Crater. After the first mile from Teakettle Junction you will cross Lost Burro Gap at 4,700 feet. Two and a half miles from the junction is the road west to the Lost Burro Mine. Bypassing this turn-off will bring you into Hidden Valley. In the spring time, after a wet winter, this valley is covered with flowers. In the southeast section of the valley is a small dry lake, which is closed to vehicles. Driving south out of this valley takes you to Ulida Flat, and Goldbelt Springs. This area provides some great panoramas of the high desert and interesting canyons with old mines to investigate. Continuing southeast will take you over Hunter Mountain and to Saline Valley Road at the top of Grapevine Canyon. Due to deep, loose gravel and some steep grades, 4-wheel drive is a must on this road.

Hole in Rock Spring (D4)

This site is a short hike described in Chapter 4. The spring is at the end of a short trail, just off Daylight Pass Road, 1¼ miles north of Hells Gate. The spring is located in a small break in the Travertine formations at the end of a small canyon. There is a half of a metal barrel inside to catch and hold the water.

Hot Spring Area (A3, A4)
This area is along a spur road northeast of the sand dunes in Saline Valley. There are actually three major springs in the area; Lower Warm Spring, Palm Spring, and Upper Warm Spring. There is almost always a small encampment of people at these springs.

The area offers camping but there are not any established campgrounds around the springs. The users of this area have proven that outdoor lovers will maintain the places they use. Previous users have even built concrete ponds to capture the hot water for a spa like effect. The bathers at the ponds are predominantly nude, but clothing is optional, this seems to be a common understanding in the area.

There are times, like winter holidays, when this area is very crowded, even though this is not an official campground. If you choose to visit this area, bring drinking water, and be prepared to be self-sufficient.

Little Hebe Crater (B2)
This volcanic crater is actually a series of three craters, inside a large crater. It is located just south of Ubehebe Crater. The craters can be reached via a ½ mile trail beginning at the parking area. This trail climbs

200 feet, although it feels like more, to the rim of the craters. Be sure to wear sturdy shoes or boots; and take your camera the views are great and worth the walk.

Like Ubehebe Crater, these craters are thought to have been formed by steam explosions rather than lava flows. There are some great photographic opportunities at this crater. Bring plenty of film and be prepared to walk.

Midway Well (C4)
This is a former campground; it was closed in 1971. The last time I was there, old picnic tables were still under some of the Mesquite trees growing in this small heavily wooded area. The well is in a steel barrel just inside the Mesquite hummocks. The area is less than 0.3 miles off the road to Scotty's Castle, and 8.4 miles north of the junction with Highway 190. This area provides excellent opportunities to photograph some now undisturbed Mesquite.

Mud Canyon (D4)
This is a wide canyon that cuts through Kit Fox Hills, east of the Sand Dunes. Daylight Pass Road is the paved route through the canyon. The low hills on either side of the road offer great examples of how water erosion has shaped the terrain of the valley. This canyon and wash is a great place to photograph flowers in the spring of each year.

Phinney Canyon (C3, D3)
This is our get away from it all canyon. You can reach it by taking the Phinney Wash Road off U.S. 95, 11.7 miles north of Beatty. This canyon lies between Grapevine Peak and Wahguyhe Peak, the two highest mountains in the Grapevine Mountains, 8,738 and 8,628 feet respectively. It is advisable to have a 4-wheel drive vehicle to explore this canyon. At the end of the canyon a short walk will bring you to Doe Spring and a great view of upper Mesquite Flat.

Racetrack Valley (B4)
The major feature of this valley is a large dry lake, measuring 3 miles long and 2 miles wide. Contrary to the name, you cannot drive on the playa of the lake bed. The lake bed is about 24 miles south of Ubehebe Crater; about 5 miles south of Teakettle Junction when you take the fork to the right. It's advisable to have a 4-wheel drive vehicle to explore this area.

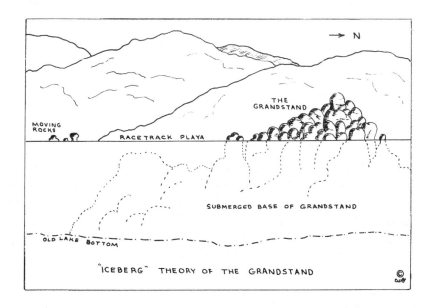

At the north end of the dry lake is a strangely carved rock formation called the Grandstand. Theory has it that this outcropping is actually just the top of a much larger rock structure going deep into the mud of the dry lake. Additional theories say that the mud is at least 1,000 feet deep.

At the south end of the dry lake is perhaps the strangest phenomenon of Death Valley. The Moving Rocks. The dry lake bed shows scarred trails left by the rocks as they move northward on the playa. Some of the rocks weigh up to 500 pounds and travel upwards of 500 yards. Dr. Sharp of the California Institute of Technology at Pasadena has been studying these rocks for many years. Dr. Sharp theorizes that if the playa gets a few centimeters of rain, and the wind is very strong the rocks actually hydroplane across the mud. The structure of the soil on the playa is such that it would make a very fine, slick mud. The wind is almost always blowing in this area, so barring anything better, Dr. Sharp's theory may be accurate.

The playa is closed to all vehicles. You will have to walk across the south end of the playa, about ½ mile from the road to see the best examples of the rocks and their tracks. Do not move or take the rocks. Take your camera, a picture of a rock and its trail in the dry mud is great evidence when you try to tell friends about this place.

117

Red Wall Canyon (C3)

Although not as narrow as Fall or Titus Canyon, this canyon is still beautiful in its own right. Just as the name implies the color of the walls is very impressive. This canyon is 3½ miles north of Titus Canyon, and is reached by hiking north along the fan from the mouth of Titus. I usually couple a visit to this canyon with a hike to Fall Canyon. Plan to take the better part of a full day to see both canyons.

Rhyolite (D3)

Even though this ghost town is outside the park boundary, its importance and relevance to Death Valley cannot be denied. During its heyday it was the largest city in the area. At the time it was the second largest city in Nevada, with a population of more than 5,000 people. Gold was the primary attraction for most of the people that lived in Rhyolite.

A gold discovery by Shorty Harris and E. L. Cross in August 1904 sparked the birth of the town. Over the few short boom years, from 1905 to 1912, there were at least 50 working mines surrounding the town. By the beginning of the 1920's the gold and all the people were gone, and Rhyolite was a ghost town.

At its peak this very metropolitan city had 3 water systems that could have supported up to 75,000 people. It also had telephone service, electricity, 3 railroad lines, 2 daily newspapers, 2 undertakers, 2 hospitals, 8 doctors, 2 dentists, 19 hotels and boarding houses, and 50 saloons. On the cultural side one could find, an opera house, a symphony, baseball team, tennis courts, and swimming pools. There was even a stock exchange, with 75 members, for investing in and trading mining shares.

Today you can visit the buildings and structures that remain on the site of the town. The most substantial structure, the Tonapah and Tidewater Railroad station, is at the end of the paved road on the east end of town. The Bureau of Land Management is taking steps to preserve this building, it is currently surrounded by a chain link fence to prevent vandalism. Other structures remaining in the town include the partial shell of the bank, a jail, the shell of the Porter store, and remnants of a school. There are numerous foundations and some partial adobe walls.

The town's most unique structure is the Bottle House, built in 1906 by Tom Kelly using about 50,000 beer and water bottles. The mortar is ac-

tually mud from the surrounding area. The roof is anchored by heavy wires that are embedded deep into the walls. The small "model" town outside the bottle house was built by a resident, Tommy Thompson, in the 1970's. The story is that he built these to entertain his grandchildren. This house was occupied until the late 1980s, when the Bureau of Land Management began its efforts to preserve the house and the area. Today the house is surrounded by a chain link fence, but a BLM volunteer is usually on hand to open the gate permitting visitors a close up look.

Just west of Rhyolite is the site of the town of Bullfrog. About all that remains here is the site of a well preserved cemetery. Even though the gold strike was at Bullfrog, its citizens eventually all moved to Rhyolite. One source said that the final blow for the town was when its last few hold-out residents actually tore down their homes and buildings, and moved them to Rhyolite. In reporting this event one of the local newspapers ran the headline "The Bullfrog Croaketh."

Rhyolite is 35 miles from Furnace Creek and 4 miles west of Beatty, Nevada. As you approach Rhyolite on Nevada Highway 374, you will see the Bullfrog Mine complex. According to some of the people in the area, they are mining both above ground, in an open pit, and through a series of underground shafts.

119

Saline Valley (A4)

This is one of the most remote places in California. There are very few roads entering or crossing this area, and there are even fewer people than there are roads. Combined with Eureka Valley there are approximately 500,000 acres of roadless and people-less land. Make sure your gas tank is full, and that you have lunch and water in your vehicle for a drive here.

While the area may seem empty to the casual visitor, those that get out and investigate all that this valley has to offer quickly find out it's not empty at all. This is probably one of the most extraordinary places on earth today. Exploring the valley leaves you with the feeling that you may be the first person to walk over the land. If you want undisturbed nature this is the place for it.

Saline Valley Road (A2, A3, A4)

This road travels up the western side of the park and connects Highway 190 in the south to Death Valley Road in the north. The road covers 89 miles. The junction of Highway 190 and Saline Valley Road is 69 miles from Furnace Creek Ranch. It is just outside the park boundary. You re-enter the park after having traveled 7.7 miles north of the junction.

The first 14 miles of the road is paved. At the end of the pavement you are at the junction to Cerro Gordo Mine and Lee Flat. Turn right to continue on to Saline Valley. This takes you through the southern end of the Lee Flat Joshua Tree Forest. You come to the junction of the Hunter Mountain and Hidden Valley road 7.1 miles from the Cerro Gordo junction. A left turn takes you down through Grapevine Canyon into Saline Valley.

Once in Saline Valley, it's a 22 mile ride to Salt Lake and the old tramway. Three miles north of the tramway is a shortcut route to the Hot Springs Area. This short cut requires 4-wheel drive. There is a better road 5 miles north of this, if you stay on Saline Valley Road to the west of the dunes. The hot springs are about 8 miles east of the main road.

The Willow Springs area is 4.6 miles north of the turn off to the hot springs, on Saline Valley Road. Talc is mined in this area, at the White Eagle and Grey Eagle mines. The Waucoba Springs are 12.3 miles further to the north. The spring is on a spur road, about ¼ mile east of the main road.

About a mile north of the spring the road enters the wooded area surrounding Whippoorwill Canyon. Another 3 miles and the road traverses Whippoorwill Flat, camping is available year-'round in this area. In another 2.5 miles you will come to Opal Canyon. The road into the canyon only goes in a little over a mile and then turns to the west. From here it heads into the first mile of Marble Canyon. At this point you are only 6.2 miles from Death Valley Road.

Salt Lake (A4)
This normally dry lake is 37.2 miles north of Highway 190 on Saline Valley Road. This area has historic importance for the production of borax and salt. Between 1888 and 1893 the Conn and Trudo Borax Company operated near this dry lake. There are still some stone foundations remaining in the area from their borax works.

Perhaps the most interesting aspect of the lake is the now abandoned salt works. This was once the Saline Valley Salt Company. It happens that this lake has exceptionally pure salt deposits, that required little or no refining. You can see the remains of the evaporator beds at the southwestern edge of the lake. Simply follow the tramway towers from the road to the lake. The tramway was used to carry salt from this lake to Swansea in the Owens Valley. The tramway is historically significant because it was

Salt Tramway Tower

121

one of the steepest ever built and operated in the United States. It is said the tramway could carry 20 tons of salt per hour. It was used off and on from 1913 until 1936. It started at 1,100 feet at the lake, rose to 8,500 feet on the crest of the Inyo Mountains, and then descended to 3,600 feet on the far end.

If you sight along the tram line, with binoculars, from the lake to the mountains you can still pick out structures on the mountains. Walking along the tramway route near the lake you can still find remnants of the cable used to haul the salt. These ruins are listed in the National Register of Historic Places. The majority of the tramway is outside the park on Bureau of Land Management and U.S. Forest Service lands.

Scotty's Castle (C2)
Without a doubt Scotty's Castle is the most photographed, written about, and visited sight in the park. Formally know as Death Valley Ranch, this home was built by Albert and Bessie Johnson, between 1922 and 1931. The castle is 53 miles north of Furnace Creek Ranch, in Grapevine Canyon.

Johnson was an investor who had grubstaked Death Valley Scotty in the past, and had traveled to the area repeatedly with him. Johnson had chronic health problems as the result of a serious accident. In the desert he made a remarkable recovery and set about building a home for himself, and his wife. The castle and surrounding buildings are an indication of the wealth Johnson had acquired. The structure also fit very well with the flamboyant lifestyle of Scotty. He would tell anyone who would listen that he was building a castle in the desert.

An error in the original land surveys caused Johnson to begin construction on land that was not actually his. Construction of the castle was halted in 1931 until the problem could be resolved. Johnson was actually able to purchase the land in 1937. The depression had cost Johnson a large portion of his wealth and thus he never was able to resume construction. The castle remains today almost exactly as it was when the construction stopped.

Johnson passed away in 1948 and Scotty continued to live in the castle until his death in 1954. His grave and that of his dog are atop Windy Hill just above the Castle. A small cross and a plaque mark the grave.

Following Johnson's death the castle was held in trust by the Gospel Foundation. They continued to operate the castle as a hotel and tourist attraction, until it was sold to the National Park Service.

The Park Service owns the castle and is directing all efforts toward preserving it and maintaining a historic atmosphere there. The staff is even wearing National Park Service uniforms that are re-creations of their circa 1930s attire. Living history tours are offered at regular intervals every day from 9:00am until 5:00pm. There is a fee for these tours. Check at the Visitor Center for current rates. The tour is worth the price just to see the opulence inside that is even grander than the outside. The castle grounds are open from 7:00am to 6:00pm. There is no charge to explore areas around the outside of the castle.

Some amazing mechanical systems were built to provide comfort to the castle residents. Behind the castle, just off the unfinished patio between the clock tower and the main building, is an evaporation cooling plant. This plant looks large enough to support one of today's medium sized office buildings. Inside the base of the clock tower is a power generating room with two water-powered generators, and a back-up diesel-powered one. The water power came from the castle's water source, Grapevine Springs, and drove Pelton type water wheels.

Stovepipe Well (C4)

Just to the north of the Sand Dune Picnic Area on the dirt road is the real Stovepipe Well. This water source was used by prospectors and travelers crossing the valley between Rhyolite and Skidoo. In the early days, the well would usually be filled over by wind blown sand. It always required some searching on the part of travelers to find the water. This was until someone marked it with a length of stove pipe that was simply stuck into the sand.

Prior to the building of Stovepipe Wells Village, a man named James Clark operated the Stovepipe Road House, at the well, serving refreshments somewhat more potent than water to travelers at the well. The building was nothing more than a covered dugout along the road.

In the 1930s, following the Depression, CCC workers built a stone platform over the well and installed a hand pump. Today, the pump remains but does not function. Looking east from the well, up into the Kit Fox Hills you may be able to pick out traces of the old wagon road that connected the two towns.

Surveyor's Well (C4)

This well was a source of water and a popular stopping point on the old road to Scotty's Castle. The well is located one mile due west of Midway Well. A trail heads west from this well to Cottonwood Canyon and Goldbelt Springs. The site of the well is marked by a single, large Cottonwood tree, one of very few trees in this part of the park.

The old roadbed adjacent to this well was built, in part, by Bob Eichbaum, the builder of Stovepipe Wells Hotel and the Death Valley Toll Road. To stimulate tourism and thus guests at his hotel, he built this road to provide access to Scotty's Castle, Ubehebe Crater and Racetrack Dry Lake.

Teakettle Junction (B4)

The road leading to either Racetrack Valley or Hidden Valley has one main junction. The origin of the name of this junction is unknown, but over the years travelers have adorned the sign with a variety of tea kettles, coffee pots and other such paraphernalia. One thing for sure you cannot miss where you are supposed to turn to get to either Racetrack Valley or Hidden Valley.

Tie Canyon (C2)

During World War II the defunct Tonopah and Tidewater Railroad was dismantled to reclaim the much needed steel for our war effort. The ties from the rail beds were purchased by Johnson and Scotty to be firewood for the castle's fireplaces. Stories have it that they paid $2,000 for the ties and $20,000 to have them shipped to the castle. There is more than a 100 year supply of firewood in the canyon. Various accounts put the number of ties stored here at anywhere from 125,000 to 250,000.

You can get a quick look at a portion of these ties from the first landing on the clock tower stairs, behind Scotty's Castle. If you want a close up look, the canyon is open for your own explorations. If you venture into the canyon be aware that rattlesnakes and other such critters like the shelter provided by the ties.

The odd structure adjacent to the ties stored here is a gravel separator used during the construction of the castle.

Titus Canyon (C3, C4, D3)

This canyon is named for Edgar Morris Titus, a tenderfoot, prospector who was last seen looking for water with some of his burros in this canyon. The only trace ever found of him was a hastily made sign he apparently left for others in his party. It said: "Hurry on I'm going down to investigate the spring. Titus." When he did not return, one of the men he was traveling with went to look for him. Theory has it that Titus and his would be rescuer friend became lost and were dying of thirst, when a third man happened upon them. This third man died, along with Titus and his partner, while trying to help them. All three men were buried in the northern part of the valley.

This outstanding canyon is probably second only to Scotty's Castle as a visitor attraction in this part of the park. The canyon can be easily driven through by any vehicle with high clearance. Often you will encounter a hardy soul gingerly picking his way through the canyon in a passenger car. It can be done, but you must be careful not to get stuck. The gravel is loose and almost liquid in some spots.

You should allow a minimum of 2½ hours to drive through the canyon. This does not count the time it takes to get to the one-way entrance road, in Nevada. Be sure to allow extra time if you are visiting the park during

Post Office At Leadfield

peak visitor periods. If you are the curious type, like me, and want to investigate everything the canyon has to offer, plan on at least 5 hours.

Check with the Park Rangers to ensure that the canyon is in fact open and passable for your vehicle. Be sure your fuel tank is full and that you have plenty of water; it might be a good idea to pack a lunch for a picnic on the way.

The entrance road is on Nevada Highway 374, 34 miles from Furnace Creek Ranch, and outside the monument boundary. The road is one way, heading west. The first 12 miles of the road cuts straight through typical Nevada high desert, sagebrush and more sagebrush. Even though it can get monotonous, keep your speed down if your vehicle is not built for this terrain, and to keep the dust down. At the end of this road is Red Pass and the beginning of the sites along Titus Canyon Road. Do take an opportunity to stop here and look around. There is a wide spot on the right!

After driving down from Red Pass, on a road that appears to be barely perched on the side of a mountain, you come to the site of Leadfield. This town was created by an infamous promoter, Charles Julian, who in 1926 charmed the world with his Western Lead Mines Company and a reputed hundred-million dollar silver-lead mine. What he was doing was blasting out tunnels in the hillsides and salting the tailings with lead ore. Investors jumped at the chance to make a quick profit and, without further investigation, began hauling construction supplies across the desert to the new town. Before the bubble burst, the town had a newspaper, post office, general store, and all the other usual businesses that flourish in a boom town. It had everything except silver or lead, and Charles Julian was also noticeably missing; he later admitted making more than a million dollars from this scam. Charles Julian was later indicted for mail fraud as the result of another scam in Oklahoma.

While at Leadfield you should take some time to look around and explore some of the remaining buildings. There are a few "Cousin Jack" houses in the area. These were brought to this country by Irish and Welsh miners as a form of cheap housing. While you are exploring, be careful not to fall into one of the many abandoned mine shafts that dot this valley. It is also a good idea to watch out for rattlesnakes and other creatures in the buildings.

As you drive down the canyon past Leadfield you will come to a sharp "S" turn in the road. A sign on your right names the nearby rock forma-

"Cousin Jack" At Leadfield

tion "When Rocks Bend." This wonder demonstrates the tremendous forces that have been at work forming this valley. This is the most dramatic of many such examples around the valley.

A short way past this sight is Klare Spring. This area always has some water as is evidenced by the tules growing along the base of the cliff. Petroglyphs can be found on the rocks above the spring. During the warm, sometimes slightly humid, springtime a particularly vicious black fly likes to hang around this water source.

A short way down the canyon from the spring, the canyon walls begin getting closer and closer. The last few miles of the canyon get quite narrow, allowing you to appreciate the beauty of the canyon walls first hand. If you can do so without impeding traffic, stop and get out of your vehicle to view the walls of the canyon towering over you. As you drive through this part of the canyon, be alert for people walking up the road from the parking lot just outside the mouth. If you were not able to stop in the canyon, you may want to take a moment and walk back into the narrowest portion. The pavement is 2½ miles from the exit of the canyon. When you reach the pavement, take a moment to look back. You will find Titus Canyon has all but disappeared.

Triangle Spring

Triangle Spring (C4)
This small spring is hidden behind the small hills west of Scotty's Castle Road 1½ miles south of Midway Well. As you drive south along the road you may catch a glimpse of the top of a Date Palm that is growing next to this spring. This spring is thought to be one of the water sources for the Arrow Weed plants at Devils Cornfield. The name for this spring originated from the fact that it, Midway Well, and Surveyors Well form a geographic triangle. The water at this spring is brackish and heavily mineralized.

Ubehebe Crater (B2)
This almost perfectly shaped volcanic crater is the result of lava or magma encountering ground water and not having a fissure to vent through. This explosive eruption took place about 3,000 years ago. The Timbisha Shoshone legends call this place "Wosa," the "Coyote's burden basket."

As you approach the crater, large black splotches can be seen scattered around the foothills of the Cottonwood Mountains, evidence of the dramatic volcanic activity. The road divides as you near the crater. Stay to the right. A one way loop brings you to the parking are immediately in front of the crater. Be prepared as you open the doors of your car; a stiff usually cold wind is always blowing in this area. Just a few feet from your car, you can look across the crater's rim to the opposite side almost a half mile away.

The parking lot side of the crater does not have a sharp drop-off. Instead a 30 degree slope leads to the bottom. There is a trail leaving from behind the interpretive sign, leading to the bottom 462 feet down. You may easily walk to the bottom, but expect some significant work walking back up the very loose volcanic ash.

The bottom of the crater is partially covered by a pool of white and red sediment. This is silt from the side walls that has been washed to the bottom by the rains. A few desert holly bushes grow on the bottom.

Val Nolan's Grave (C4)
This grave is near the intersection of Scotty's Castle Road and the Sand Dune Picnic Area dirt road. "A Victim Of The Elements," this epitaph is more than true in this case. Little is known about Val "Shorty" Nolan

Val Nolan's Grave

except that he was last seen alive on July 31, 1931, in Rhyolite, on his way to prospect in Death Valley. His body was found and buried by a movie crew on November 6, 1931.

Wagon Wheel History (C4)
Abandoned roads take a long time to disappear in the desert. An interpretive sign is on the west side of Scotty's Castle Road, just south of the Sand Dune Picnic Area Road. Stand at the sign and look west toward Stovepipe Well. You can see the wheel tracks of the Rhyolite-Skidoo Road. Turn around facing east, you can see more, very faint, tracks leading up into a canyon in the Kit Fox Hills. Stovepipe Well was a water and rest stop on this road. As of this writing, these tracks are about 90 years old.

Chapter 7
Center Park

Area

The northern edge of this area of the park is an imaginary line that crosses the park, east to west, at the Sand Dunes in Death Valley. The eastern and western boundaries are the park boundaries themselves. The southern limit of the area is another imaginary line crossing the park just south of Artist's Palette.

This is the area where visitors with a limited amount of time to spend in the Park will want to concentrate their activities. This is where a majority of the historic and scenic areas of the park are found. It offers widely diverse topography and geology from salt flats to pine forests, and at times snow capped peaks.

The main route through this area is California Highway 190. The majority of areas important to visitors in this area are accessible by either paved roads or well graded dirt roads.

Favorite Places

Salt Creek is at the top of my list of favorite places in this section of the park. Finding this much water, salty or otherwise, in the middle of the country's driest, hottest desert is an enigma. And to find fish here just adds to the sense of wonder.

I usually go to the Visitor Center many times during every trip to the park. This is where I get answers to my many questions. I also like checking out the exhibits or talking about changes in the park with the center staff. Be sure to see the museum and the interpretive presentations. Also if you like guided walks, don't forget to pick up a schedule of these.

Zabriskie Point, which overlooks the Badlands and Manly Beacon, is the place I go to watch the colors of the landscape change with the rising sun. On a clear spring morning you can watch the color go all the way from dull gray, to pink, to golden, and finally to a light tan in the course of about two hours.

Death Valley - Central

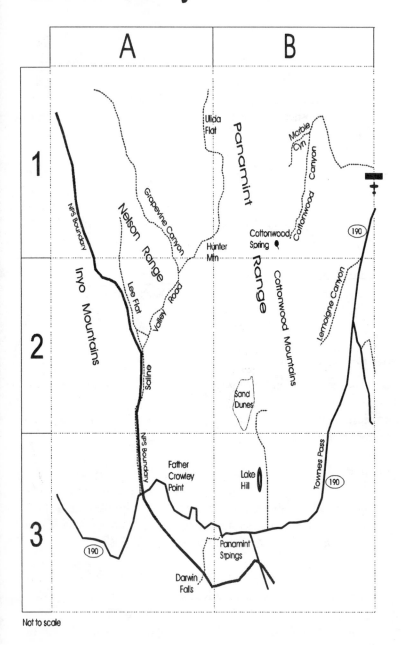

Not to scale

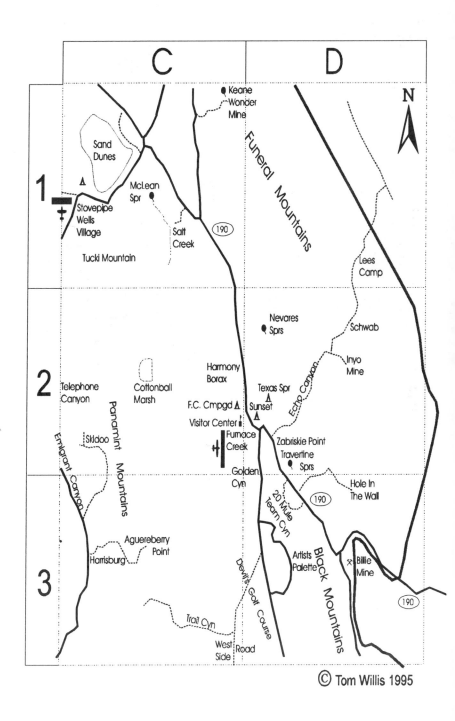

C

D

N

Keane
Wonder
Mine

Funeral Mountains

Sand
Dunes

1

McLean
Spr

Stovepipe
Wells
Village

Salt
Creek

190

Lees
Camp

Tucki Mountain

Nevares
Sprs

Schwab

Telephone
Canyon

Cottonball
Marsh

Harmony
Borax

Inyo
Mine

2

Texas Spr

Echo Canyon

F.C. Cmpgd

Sunset

Panamint Mountains

Visitor Center

Furnace
Creek

Zabriskie Point

Emigrant Canyon

Skidoo

Travertine
Sprs

Golden
Cyn

Hole In
The Wall

190

20 Mule Team Cyn

Aguereberry
Point

3

Harrisburg

Devil's Golf Course

Artists
Palette

Black Mountains

Billie
Mine

190

Trail Cyn

West
Side Road

© Tom Willis 1995

133

To See and Do

Aguereberry Point (C3)

Here is a wonderful overlook on the west side of Death Valley, this point is just southwest of Furnace Creek. It provides a bird's eye view of the central part of the valley. There is a mountain just south of the point that blocks the view of the southern valley and salt flat.

This point is named for Jean Pierre "Pete" Aguereberry, the co-founder of Harrisburg. He and Shorty Harris discovered a ledge of gold, set their claim markers, and agreed to name the town that was sure to grow "Harrisberry." The town did grow, but since everybody knew Shorty, and Aguereberry was a stranger to most, the name of the town quickly evolved to Harrisburg.

Aguereberry Point

When the gold veins ran out, the people left and took most of the town with them. Pete Aguereberry stayed on to work a small mine. He continued to work his "Eureka" mine earning a modest living until his death in November 1945.

Bob Eichbaum built a road suitable for automobiles and would take guests from his Stovepipe Wells Hotel to the point. Eichbaum called the point "Grand View." This was one of his attempts to offer attractions similar to those of his competitors at Furnace Creek Inn, who offered their guests Dante's View. The Automobile Club of Southern California actually named the point in honor of Pete Aguereberry in the mid-1930s.

The point is off the road to Wildrose Canyon 11.9 miles from Emigrant Canyon. Turn east onto a graded, but often dusty, dirt road. Follow this for 6 miles to the overlook. For the clearest view it is best to get to the point early in the day. Heat created haze can be a problem in the afternoon. Binoculars are a real plus here for identifying the sites below. The green square surrounded by all the white and gray is Furnace Creek Ranch.

Artist's Palette (D3)
The one-way paved road through this area begins 10 miles south of Furnace Creek Ranch off Badwater Road. This road is not recommended for buses, large motorhomes, or vehicles towing trailers. There are turnouts along Artist's Drive that allow you to park and explore the colorful canyons that are in this area.

About 4½ miles up Artists Drive you will find the parking area for Artist's Palette. The palette is across a canyon from the parking area. The

Artist's Palette

best way to see this area is to get out of your vehicle and climb some of the small hills around the parking lot.

The best time of the day, to get the full rich colors that have made this area famous, is mid to late afternoon. The colored deposits will reflect the afternoon sun since they have a full western exposure. It seems the lower the angle of the sun the better the colors are. I have found a wide angle lens is a great camera option here to get the best pictures.

The road back out to the highway winds its way down "Artist's Wash." Here the road is sometimes paved, but mostly it's narrow and covered with dirt. This portion of the road is why it is not recommended for large vehicles. Just across the highway from the end of Artist's Drive is a raided mound called a turtleback, it is a low angle fault scarp.

Borax Haystacks (C3)

As discussed in the day hikes in Chapter 4, this area is where the Chinese laborers piled borax to prove claim assessment work for Harmony Borax Works. Today what remains are about 15 square miles of small mounds. It is unclear what each mound represented other than some specific amount of borate that was removed for processing at nearby Harmony.

Borax Haystacks

Depending on the amount of recent rainfall, there can be a considerable amount of water on the salt flat between the Haystacks and Harmony Borax Works. The ground water and rainfall combine to keep this entire area very damp or soggy for much of the visitor season.

Borax Museum (C3)
This small museum is located at the back of the main parking lot of Furnace Creek Ranch. The building that houses the museum was originally built in 1883 as a bunkhouse, kitchen and office for the Monte Blanco Mine. It was moved from 20-Mule Team Canyon in 1954 by the Pacific Coast Borax Company to its present location. It has been a museum ever since. The admission is free.

The exterior of the building has been preserved exactly as it appeared when it was in 20-Mule Team Canyon. This includes the 8 foot wide porch that completely encircles the building. The displays inside include an extensive mineral display, collections of mining, railroad, and mule team memorabilia. Do not miss the collection that is out back. Here you will find all sorts of large items including stagecoaches and wagons, an oxen shoeing rig, a 20 Mule Team barn, a complete 2-6-0 steam locomotive from the Death Valley Railroad, and much more.

Locomotive At Borax Museum

Burned Wagons Point (C1)
In December 1849, shortly after entering the valley with the Bennett-Arcane wagon party, a group of single men called the Jayhawkers headed north by themselves. After about three days they camped near the head waters of Salt Creek. They decided to burn their wagons to smoke some meat from the oxen they slaughtered. This group then walked out of the valley by way of what is now called Townes Pass and Jayhawker Canyon. Getting to the site is another day hike described in Chapter 4.

A historical monument stands on the shoulder of Highway 190 at Stove-pipe Wells Village, indicating that this site is near by. Actually, it is about five miles from the location of the marker.

Cottonball Marsh (C2)
This is the site where Aaron and Rosie Winters discovered borax in Death Valley. W. T. Coleman bought their claim for $20,000, after Winters sent ore samples to his company for assay. The site of Westside Borax Camp can be found to the west of the marsh on the edge of the salt pan. The area between this marsh and Harmony Borax Works is where the Chinese laborers gathered the raw borates for purification. See the details in Chapter 4 for a day hike trip to this area.

This is the most extensive marsh on the Death Valley salt pan. The marsh also is home to its own species of pupfish, *Cyprinodon milleri*. The springs that feed the marsh are located on the west side of Cottonball Basin. The water in the marsh is usually 12 to 18 inches deep, and is much saltier than the ocean. A chemical analysis indicates the water in this spring may travel through faults from as far away as Mesquite Springs.

Cottonwood / Marble Canyons (B1)
These two canyons are in the Cottonwood Mountains. The canyons are favorites for 4-wheel drive enthusiasts. Although they are not difficult trips, 4-wheel drive is required because of the deep sand and gravel encountered along the way. The landscape is unequaled anywhere in the valley. (See chapter 4)

Cottonwood Canyon is a true paradox. Amid this arid landscape, we have a real oasis complete with a tree lined stream. Cottonwood Spring and Creek provide a water source for many animals calling the Cottonwood Mountains home, including the Desert Bighorn Sheep.

A back country trip to these canyons starts at the north end of the Stove-pipe Wells Village Airstrip. About 5 miles out on this sandy road you will come to a fork. Go right. The old road on the left is closed to vehicles. In another 3 miles you will enter a set of narrows that marks the beginning of Cottonwood Canyon. At this point the track you have been following may disappear. Follow this canyon until it opens up onto a flat. You will come to a sign that directs you to Marble Canyon and Goldbelt Springs. Following the road to the right will take you into Marble Canyon. Larger vehicles will have to stop in a couple of miles as the canyon becomes very narrow. Smaller rigs will be able to go about another ¾ mile before reaching a large boulder that blocks the entire canyon.

Returning from Marble Canyon or staying to the left at the sign will put you on the road to Cottonwood Spring. About 4.2 miles up the canyon from the sign look for a large cave eroded out of the side of the canyon. The canyon road ends about 3 miles beyond the cave. The road is blocked by tree trunks and debris washed down from the small forest that grows along Cottonwood Creek. Do take the time to hike through the cotton-wood trees to the spring. The peaceful sound of water in the small stream is great after listening to a vehicle engine for the last 2 or 3 hours.

It is possible to hike up Cottonwood Canyon to Goldbelt Springs and Hunter Mountain. From there it is possible to continue on to Racetrack Valley or over Hunter Mountain into Saline Valley.

Darwin Falls (A3)
A trip to Darwin Falls is one of the day hikes described in Chapter 4. This year round stream and 20-foot high falls are the water source for Panamint Springs Resort and the town of Darwin. It is not possible to hike all the way through the canyon, the steep rock walls around the falls should only be attempted by experienced climbers.

This oasis has cottonwood and willow trees. If you are visiting the area during the late spring a hike to these falls provides a very refreshing break. If you want to visit the pool at the top of the falls, you can continue on the Darwin Canyon Road past the turn off to the falls. The road will continue for about 5½ miles and then enter Darwin Canyon. Follow the canyon to the cabins, trees and pool at China Garden.

Devil's Cornfield (C1)

As you drive along Highway 190, east of the sand dunes the scene is reminiscent of the mid-west at harvest time. From a distance, these Arrow Weed plants resemble shocks of harvested corn. The strange plant formations have developed from strong winds eroding the soil in this area.

The large, willow-like plants are sometimes found growing several feet above the ground, held aloft by their root systems. The roots prevent the soil within them from being eroded; thus giving the larger plants the appearance of having been forced up out of the ground. The water source for these plants is thought to be Triangle Spring to the north. Walking among the plants can quickly fill your shoes with sand. The surface of the soil has a thin crust in some areas that gives way causing your foot to sink into the soft sand below.

Echo Canyon (D2)

This is a drive-through canyon, with the trip described in Chapter 4. It does require a high clearance vehicle even if you do not plan on taking the complete drive through trip. Drive carefully because the gravel can get deep in some places. If you remember not to make sudden stops and starts, you should be to avoid getting stuck.

Arrow Weed At Devil's Cornfield

There are some attractions in the canyon that do not require the complete trip through this canyon. The first is Needles Eye, sometimes called Window Rock. This rock formation is 4½ miles from the pavement of Highway 190. This is a natural window eroded in a spire on the east side of the canyon. You can climb up to the opening and will find that it's more than 9 feet tall.

About 9 miles from the pavement is the site of Inyo Mine. Gold was discovered here in 1905 and production started in 1906, but the financial panic of 1907 halted any concentrated efforts. The mine was worked off and on, mostly off, until 1940. The two key factors in the mine's demise were a lack of water and economical transportation.

This area is a well preserved outdoor museum. Adventurers taking the time to explore this area can spend some time looking at the buildings, machinery, and mining paraphernalia left behind over the years. But remember take only photos and leave only footprints.

Emigrant Canyon (B2, C3)
This is another drive-through canyon that most visitors simply take for granted as they drive to Skidoo, Harrisburg, or Wildrose. This canyon does offer some remarkable examples of the area's geologic makeup.

Burro In Emigrant Canyon

141

About 6½ miles from the Emigrant Junction turn off you will find the remnants of an ore processing facility. The cisterns here were used to leach the precious metals from crushed ore using a cyanide mixture. There was a small stamp mill immediately adjacent to these cisterns when this plant was in operation. The ground in the area is still covered with the powder like remnant of the ore after its processing was completed.

Near where Emigrant Canyon Road meets Highway 190 is the Emigrant Ranger Station. This stone building and the restroom facility across the road were build by the CCC workers in the 1930's. Fresh water, a pay telephone and a small picnic area are available here. The last time I was here the small campground, indicated on some maps, was closed. I was unable to determine whether or not it will re-open in the future.

Father Crowley Point (A3)
This monument and overlook on Highway 190 is very near the western boundary of the park. It is 63.3 miles from Furnace Creek Ranch and 8.2 miles west of Panamint Springs Resort. Be sure to drive to the end of the road beyond the monument, the overlook is 1400 feet above the floor of Rainbow Canyon. From here you have an excellent bird's eye view of Panamint Valley, The Dunes, and the western side of the Panamint Mountains.

Father Crowley was a Catholic priest living in Lone Pine. During the 1930s, he frequently traveled to Death Valley to give Sunday services for the young men at the CCC camps. He was killed in an automobile accident near Inyokern in 1940. I believe that this site of inspiration and beauty was dedicated to him by the people of the area to whom he brought the word of God.

Furnace Creek Inn (D2)
This luxury resort is located at the junction of Badwater Road and Highway 190. The resort was built by Pacific Coast Borax Company in 1926. It was initially planned for the use of borax company employees and customers, but was put to commercial use shortly after being opened.

In 1927, Union Pacific Railroad included a one night stay at the inn as part of a two day package tour of Death Valley. Their brochure stated that the inn offered 12 double occupancy rooms. The brochure went on to say that the Inn was built from adobe bricks made by Panamint Indians.

142

The complete two day package, including meals and train fare from Crucero, California, cost $42.00 per person.

At the north end of the Inn property is a stone marker dedicated to Steve Esteves. He was the head stonemason for Pacific Coast Borax Company and was responsible for the beautiful stonework at the Inn and Ranch.

Furnace Creek Ranch (D2)
This area was first inhabited, during the winter, by Timbisha Shoshone Indians. They harvested the Mesquite beans from the bushes that grew here. In the summer these people moved to the Panamint Mountains to escape the heat. The descendants of these people still reside in the Indian Village just south of the ranch.

In the early 1870s, Andy Laswell, also known as "Bellerin' Teck" or Teck Bennett, was the first white man to farm the area. He grew alfalfa, barley, and quail for sale to the miners in Panamint City. When the mining at Panamint City declined Bennett left his ranch and the valley.

In the 1880s, the ranch was taken over to grow feed and serve as a repair station for the borax wagons. At that time it was known as Greenland Ranch and Jim Dayton was the manager. In 1889, the ranch property along with Harmony Borax Works was deeded to the Pacific Coast Borax Company after W. T. Coleman filed bankruptcy. It was then renamed Furnace Creek Ranch by Francis Marion Smith, owner of the company.

There are many stories about how the Date Palms at Furnace Creek Ranch got there. But probably the most believable one is that the Department of Agriculture planted them in the 1920s to get pest free nursery stock. In 1927 there were about 125 trees at the ranch. The environment at the ranch is ideal for dates and any pests brought in with the original stock would have been hard pressed to migrate to other farm lands. If you've never eaten a natural date, I highly recommend it. The dates grown here are nothing like the sticky, gooey mess you get in a box at the grocery store. Today, there are about 1800 trees in the grove.

Golden Canyon (D2)
This canyon is just 3 miles south of Furnace Creek Ranch on Badwater Road. The canyon can best be seen if you follow the self guided tour.

A tour pamphlet is available at the parking area just off the road. My favorite time to visit the canyon is in the late afternoon, this provides the best color on the face of Red Cathedral near the end of the main trail. The afternoon sun also accents the canyon walls to a deep golden color.

Grapevine Canyon (A1)
This drive-through canyon is on the Saline Valley Road. The canyon is in the Nelson Range and provides access from Panamint Valley to Saline Valley. The road can be traveled in a high clearance vehicle. In early 1995, the dirt road in the canyon was being maintained (graded) by Inyo County road crews. The road, in the canyon, looks as if it could be very difficult to navigate without 4-wheel drive when it is wet.

About mid-way through the canyon, there is a lone Pinyon Pine tree nestled in a small niche in the steep hill along side the road. In March 1995, there was still a small amount of snow around this tree; generally a great picture; if you have color film with you!

At the southern end of the canyon is a road heading east, which takes you to Hunter Mountain and beyond. This route requires a 4-wheel drive vehicle. Along this route you will find Goldbelt Springs, Ulida Flat, and Hidden Valley. (See Hidden Valley in Chapter 6.)

Grotto Canyon

Grotto Canyon (C1)

This is a hiking canyon. You reach it by a somewhat rough dirt road 3 miles east of Stovepipe Wells Village. This road climbs the fan for about a mile before dropping down into the wash leading to the mouth of the canyon. If you are not driving a 4-wheel drive vehicle stop before you enter the wash. The gravel is deep and loose. There is a large rock on the right side of the road marking the entrance to the wash.

From where you enter the wash the first and most significant grotto is just over a mile. The last time I was in the canyon you could climb through this grotto and get into more of the canyon. From season to season the amount of gravel in the grottos varies and repeated visits over the years have made each trip a new exploration.

Grotto Canyon is one of the few places where I regularly find rattlesnakes sunning themselves on the gravel in the middle of the wash. Be careful whether you are walking or driving. I once stopped my vehicle in this canyon to take a closer look at one thing or another and my passenger found a rattlesnake right where her feet were supposed to go when she got out. She stopped in time; none-the-less she was not impressed with the situation and my choice of parking places.

Harmony Borax Works (C2)

This is the site of the first successful borax production facility in the valley. It was built by William T. Coleman after he bought the rights to the claim filed by Aaron Winters. The "cottonball" borax was harvested by Chinese laborers on the salt flat to the west of this site. This facility was operational from 1883 to 1888 and produced 20 million pounds of high grade borax.

The famous 20-Mule Team wagons were designed and built originally to haul 36½ tons of processed borax from this location to Mojave, 165 miles away. One of the remaining sets of original wagons is on display at this site.

About all that remains of the borax works today is the boiler and some of its surrounding structure and a vessel for mixing the cottonball with hot water from the boiler. The tanks used for separating and crystallizing the purified borax are long gone. The boiler was fired with Mesquite that was cut from the extensive growths around the Furnace Creek area. Local

Indians were employed to cut the wood and work the boiler. There are some excellent pictures, of the plant in operation, on interpretive signs along the trail around the works.

The building remnants to the north of the works were a part of the overall operation. The largest of the two was the superintendent's office and residence. The one-way road that leads to these structures continues on to Mustard Canyon.

During the summers Harmony Borax Works was shut down and production was moved to the Amargosa Works near Tecopa. Harmony was closed in 1888 after borax production was started near Calico. W. T. Coleman and Company filed bankruptcy in 1888 and all of his operations were deeded over to Pacific Coast Borax Company in 1889.

Harrisburg (C3)
Little, except some dirt roads and abandoned mines, remain of the town that once existed here. It was normal to tear down your building or home and take it with you when the money or gold ran out. Even if you didn't someone else would, due to the cost of shipping lumber and materials to the area.

Loading Wagons At Harmony - Circa 1880

Harrisburg is 47 miles from the visitor center, on the way to Wildrose Canyon. The site is about 2 miles from the paved road by way of the dirt road to Aguereberry Point.

Hole In The Wall (D3)

This is a 4-wheel drive trip that begins in a wash near 20-Mule Team Canyon on Highway 190. The trip starts 5 miles east of Furnace Creek Inn. A small sign on the north side of the highway says "Hole in the Wall - Jeep Trail."

About 3½ miles into the wash, you will come to a natural rock wall almost 400 feet high. A small gap in this wall provides access to the desert beyond, hence the name Hole in the Wall. This wall is one of the many geologic wonders of the valley. The texture of the rock face tells us it is sedimentary rock, but the earthquake forces along the Furnace Creek fault have caused the layers to be raised to an almost vertical position. If that were not enough the rock wall has hundreds, if not thousands, of small depressions or holes eroded into it. The overall effect provides for some very interesting photographs.

Driving through the "hole" into the valley beyond is unproductive as far as scenery goes. You will find the road does not go very far beyond this point.

Keane Wonder Mill and Mine (C1)

This mine was discovered by Jack Keane in 1903. The mill, which is the portion of the operation visited by most people, was built in 1907 by the mine's new owner Homer Wilson. The mine itself is high in the cliffs, one mile from the mill. The two were connected by an elaborate tramway that used gravity to operate and also was used to supply mechanical power to the mill. The mill housed 20 stamps and was capable of processing up to 1800 tons of ore a month. The mine and mill produced about $1,100,000 before the vein ran out in 1917.

One of the more colorful stories of this mine is that visitors were sometimes offered a chance to ride to the mine in the empty ore buckets, saving them the walk up the steep mountain. The visitors taking advantage of the offer usually found walking much less stressful after the first ride. Another story is that the cook at the mine would sometimes send deserts down to the workers at the mill via the tramway.

Keane Wonder Mill

The dirt road to Keane Wonder Mill is on the east side of the Beatty Cut-off Road, 6 miles north of the junction with Highway 190. It is 3 miles from the pavement to the parking area below the mill. The road can usually be traveled by a passenger car. All the trails around the mill site are closed to vehicles.

At this site it's a good idea to keep an eye on children who like to explore on their own. The Park Service has done a good job placing cable screens over some of the more apparent mine shafts but you never know what a child can find.

Lake Hill (B3)

This small hill was once an island in the lake that filled Panamint Valley. If you take the short ride out to the area east of The Dunes, this hill will be on the left side of the road. The elevation of the summit of Lake Hill is 2050 feet, it rises 500 feet above the dry lake bed.

Lee Flat (A2)

This area is to the north of Saline Valley Road, 12½ miles north of Highway 190. It is home to the Lee Flat Joshua Tree Forest. To reach the flat take the left fork at the junction of Saline Valley Road and Cerro

Gordo Road 8.3 miles north of Highway 190. Drive carefully in this area. I have encountered range cattle on the road more than once.

Lemoigne Canyon (B2)
This canyon was named for Jean Lemoigne, a French mining engineer. He had a small silver-lead mine and cabin at the end of the canyon. The road to the canyon requires a 4-wheel drive vehicle. It begins about 6 miles west of Stovepipe Wells Village on the north side of Highway 190. As a result of the Wilderness Act, the road is closed to vehicles 5 miles in from the highway.

In the main canyon the walls begin to close in. You will find a few dry cascades and some great rock formations along the way. Near the end of the trail the canyon forks. The right fork goes about a ½ mile past an old ore chute and ends in a box canyon. The left fork goes up to the mine and Lemoigne's cabin. The trail ends at his mine about another ¼ mile beyond the cabin.

McLean Spring (C1)
This spring is the source of the majority of water in the above ground portion of Salt Creek. There is a small waterfall, about two feet high, leading from the spring to the creek. This water was the source of the salt

used by the Jayhawkers to cure and smoke the meat of their oxen, prior to leaving the valley. Burned Wagons Point is less than a half mile away from the spring. A hike described in Chapter 4 includes a side trip to this spring. A couple of old maps I've looked at have called this spring, Jayhawker Well.

Mosaic Canyon (C1)
This canyon is a day hike described in Chapter 4. Even though some of the rock formations in this canyon have been covered over by gravel. The canyon remains one of my favorite places to walk.

Be sure to take a close look at the formations in the canyon walls. As you walk up and down the canyon the variations of the canyon walls make it seem like you are walking in a series of different canyons, rather than just one. The best time to explore and photograph the canyon is at mid-day, this way the sunlight can penetrate the narrow portions and you can capture the full beauty of the formations.

Mustard Canyon (C2)
This short drive-through canyon is on the one-way road beginning at the side of the parking lot at Harmony Borax Works. The unusual yellow

Salt Creek Waterfall

mud that forms the canyon is the source of the name. A closer look at the terrain in this canyon reveals some interesting salt and borax crystal formations.

Niter Beds (B1)
These beds of mud and clay lie off the southwest corner of Mesquite Flat. The assortment of large and small mounds are randomly placed and are completely natural. Niter is defined as native Nitrate of Soda. However, a chemical analysis of some samples did not reveal the presence of any nitrates.

You can reach the beds by hiking north, on the dirt road, from the Stovepipe Wells Village airstrip. This is the road to Cottonwood Canyon, follow it for about 2 miles. As the dirt road turns west watch carefully for an old dirt track that will take you northwest to the edge of the fan at the base of the Cottonwood Mountains. About 6 miles north of where you left the dirt road, this track also turns west. At this point you are at the southern edge of the beds; another 3 miles along the track brings you right into the beds themselves.

Panamint Springs Resort (B3)
This small motel, restaurant, and campground are on the western side of the park, on Highway 190, at the foot of the Inyo Mountains. The resort got its start in the 1930s when a local miner's wife began preparing meals for other miners and travelers in Panamint Valley.

At the time of printing, the resort offered 13 quiet, comfortable motel rooms, a small cafe, gasoline and propane, a campground with and without hookups, and an airstrip. About the only thing Panamint Springs does not offer is a public telephone; this is not their fault, the phone company doesn't come out here. It does provide an excellent base for exploring all that the Panamint, Saline, and Eureka Valleys have to offer. The resort is open year round. See Chapter 5 for additional information.

Salt Creek (C1)
This year round, below sea level creek is located just 14 miles north of the Visitor Center. A well graded dirt road takes you the 1½ miles from the pavement to the parking area, at the south end of the creek. A boardwalk, beginning at the end of the parking lot, parallels the main creek bed for a considerable distance. The Park Service adds more and more to this

as the funding becomes available. This boardwalk gives almost every visitor the chance to get close to the water. Keep in mind that this is a fragile and protected area. Please, stay on the boardwalk.

This creek is home to the famous pupfish. Everyone comes here to see them. But if you're not here in the spring, March or later, you won't see the pupfish. The fish spend much of the year in aestivation (summer hibernation) under the mud of the creek. When the fish are visible you can see them from nearly every spot on the boardwalk.

The salt tolerant grass that grows all along the creek is Pickleweed. The blades of this grass are jointed and appear to be made of a series of small beads. Breaking one of these small beads off and crushing it in your teeth will demonstrate just how tolerant this grass is to its environment.

Sand Dunes (C1)
A short, well-graded dirt road, 6.2 miles east of Stovepipe Wells Village provides access to the central dune area. The Sand Dune Picnic Area located on the road provides a good point for starting your exploration of the dunes. This is a day use area. Be sure to check with the Park Service before planning evening or night photography from this location.

Hiking into the dunes from the picnic area provides excellent opportunities to see that the sand is not as barren as you might think. There are lots of Mesquite and other plants growing right in the sand dunes. Take some time to carefully investigate the area around some of the accessible plant bases. The number of animal tracks is amazing. Do not put your hands into holes or behind large plants. You may wake up something that is not very friendly when startled.

Skidoo (C2)
This former mining town is pretty much in the same condition as Harrisburg, but determined investigation can lead you to the few structures that remain in the canyons. There is an abandoned 15 stamp mill, complete with stamps, in one of the canyons. Be careful driving the many dirt roads that cover the area, there are more old mines than you can count.

The actual site of Skidoo is little more than a Park Service sign identifying the location. Skidoo is 44 miles from the Visitor Center on a dirt road off Emigrant Canyon Road.

Stovepipe Wells Village (C1)

Stovepipe Wells Village was the first resort enterprise started in Death Valley. It was opened in November 1926 by Bob Eichbaum. Eichbaum was the builder of the first electric generating plant in Rhyolite in 1906. He formed his vision of a resort in the area of the Sand Dunes while prospecting in Death Valley after the decline of Rhyolite.

To bring his dream to reality, he had to build a road from Darwin Canyon, on the west side of Panamint Valley, to Death Valley. This was the Death Valley Toll Road, which Eichbaum completed in the summer of 1926. Old timers have told us the Death Valley toll gate stood where the hotel lobby is today. The toll was $2.00 per car and $0.50 per passenger. Trucks were charged between $4.50 and $6.50 per ton.

To meet his competition and offer his guests more access to the attractions of the northern and western valley, Eichbaum had to continue his road building efforts. He built the roads to Scotty's Castle, Ubehebe Crater, Racetrack Valley, and Aguereberry Point.

The village is 24 miles from the Visitor Center and offers motel rooms, restaurant, cocktail lounge, gift shop, general store, gasoline, a swimming pool, and a limited number of RV sites with hook-ups. See Chapter 5 for more information.

Tour Bus - Circa 1930

153

Telephone Canyon (B2)

This short canyon is a day hike described in Chapter 4. This canyon gained its name by being the route for the telephone line that connected Rhyolite and Skidoo. The telephone company was the Tucki Consolidated Telephone and Telegraph Company formed by Bob Montgomery, investor and founder of Skidoo.

The Dunes (B2)

These sand dunes are located in the very north end of Panamint Valley. You can see them as you drive along Highway 190 through the valley. Very few visitors attempt to get to The Dunes, because there is only one road into this part of the park and it misses the dunes by three miles. The Dunes are probably as close to undisturbed as you will find anywhere.

The floor of northern Panamint Valley is a large dry lake bed. The only irregularity on this playa is Lake Hill. The Dunes here are the result of winds carrying sand from the south meeting the face of the Nelson Range. There do not appear to be any cross winds, which may explain the more rounded appearance of these dunes. See Chapter 4 for directions.

Townes Pass (B3)

This steep pass on Highway 190 was named for Captain Towne, one of the original forty-niners. It was over this pass that the Jayhawkers are said to have left the valley. This pass is sometimes called Townsend Pass.

If you are driving a large motorhome or pulling a trailer, be advised that this route is very steep. The grades will tax the capabilities of all but the most powerful rigs. There are tanks of radiator water placed at turn-outs along this route. On warm days, do not use the air-conditioner in your vehicle; it will just increase your chances of over-heating your engine.

Travertine Springs (D2)

This is the main water source for the irrigation of the date palms, the golf course, and the lawns and trees of Furnace Creek Inn and Ranch. The springs are in Furnace Creek Wash, less than a mile from the Inn. They are identified by three or four large Date Palms that can be seen in a small canyon just off the north side of the highway. The water is channeled from here to the Inn and then on to the Ranch across the highway. There are 10 springs that make up Travertine Springs, combined they provide about 850 gallons of water per minute. Technically these are hot springs. The water temperature is slightly more than 70 degrees.

Tucki Mountain (C2)
This is the geologic formation that causes the sand dunes to be where they are in Death Valley. This massive mountain rises 6730 feet above the valley floor, almost directly behind Stovepipe Wells Village. The gold mining area around Skidoo is on a high plateau at the south side of Tucki Mountain.

Some limited silver mining activity took place at various sites on Tucki Mountain, but no significant silver deposits were found. One claim filed by the Nossano brothers, Jasper and Joseph, was reported to have shown masses of silver in its assay samples. Some prospectors and investors were certain this was the famed Lost Gunsight Mine. Even if it wasn't, the legend helped the brothers sell their claim for $70,000.

20 Mule Team Canyon (D3)
This drive through canyon is just off Highway 190, 5½ miles east of Furnace Creek Ranch. This canyon was the original home of the Borax Museum building. The site of the Monte Blanco borax mine was in the hills around this canyon.

Borax Prospect At 20 Mule Team Canyon

Today, as you drive through the canyon you will see a number of borate prospects. The small mine tunnels were dug by prospectors looking for borax. The old tunnels are unstable and are best looked at from outside their entrances.

Visitor Center (C2)

This has been our point of reference, or starting point, for most of the things we have discussed about the park. The center also serves as the Park Service Headquarters. It is a must-see place for everyone visiting Death Valley. It has a little of everything, exhibits, artifacts, history, information, books, maps, and interpretive presentations. A stop at the visitor center is always time well spent, you should be sure that it is part of your plans.

Officially, it is known as the Horace M. Albright Visitor Center and Death Valley Museum. Mr. Albright was born in Bishop, California in 1890. He was an Assistant Director working for Stephen Mather at the Park Service in the early 1930s. He was appointed Director after Mather left, and was instrumental in getting President Hoover to sign the proclamation making Death Valley a National Monument.

Zabriskie Point (D2)

This overlook is 4½ miles east of the Visitor Center. There is a large parking area off the highway. You will have to walk up a short hill to the overlook. At the top is a stunning view of the Badlands, Gower Gulch, and Manly Beacon.

The Badlands are the hills surrounding the point. These unusual hills are formations left by the receding waters of Lake Manly.

The point is named for Christian Brevoort Zabriskie, a superintendent of Pacific Coast Borax Company at Columbus Marsh. Gower Gulch, the small canyon winding through the Badlands, was named for George T. Gower. Manly Beacon, an unmistakable 823 foot rock monolith, was named for William Lewis Manly.

The colors of the landscape may appear to be a drab and lifeless series of tans and browns in the afternoon sun. They really come to life in the morning sun, at times Manly Beacon will appear to be the world's largest

gold nugget. I have heard people describe the Badlands as resembling vanilla ice cream topped with dark chocolate.

Zabriskie Point and its surroundings always provide visitors with some excellent opportunities for unusual photographs. The best light conditions exist in the early morning when you have the most contrast in the colors of the mud hills of the Badlands and the best color on Manly Beacon. This is another place where I've gotten my best pictures with a wide angle lens.

If you are adventurous you can walk down Gower Gulch to Golden Canyon. This is an easy walk but as always be sure to take water with you. Golden Canyon is about 3½ miles away. Along the way you will find many more photo opportunities.

Mosaic Canyon "Whirlpool" (1972)

Chapter 8
Southern Park

Area

This last area of the park starts at another imaginary line that is just south of Artist's Palette and encompasses the remainder of the park to the south. With the exception of a few sites this area is visited only by a small portion of the people who come to the park each year. Perhaps this is due to the lack of services in the area.

When you visit this area be advised that gasoline, food, or other services are not available along the roads between Furnace Creek Ranch and Shoshone or Tecopa. Be sure your gas tank and water supply are both full before you embark on your trip south.

The southern part of the park does offer elements that are just as impressive and wondrous as those found in the other areas. The distances between sites are no greater that those encountered with other sites. If you are traveling with children in the car, take along some things to entertain them. Some of the scenery in this area will test a youngster's span of attention.

Favorite Places

My favorite place in this part of the park is Butte Valley. I like sitting on the bluff near the Geologist's Cabin, looking out over the valley and taking in the grandeur of Striped Butte. I really envy Carl Mengel, a miner that lived and worked a mine in this valley.

I regularly visit Badwater. I particularly like being here early in the morning as the sun begins to light the top of Telescope Peak. I sometimes enjoy sitting on the steps and watching the sun rise until the Panamint Mountains are bathed in sunlight all the way down to their base at the salt pan.

I also like the ghost town of Ballarat. Even though it's outside the park, I put this area in the same category as Rhyolite; the residents of the town contributed to the history of the park.

Death Valley - South

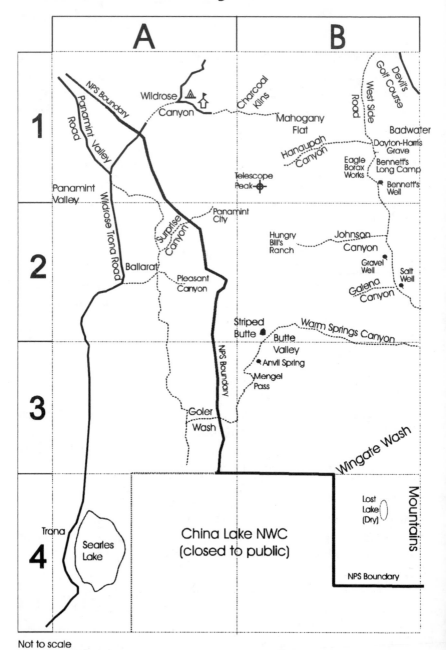

Not to scale

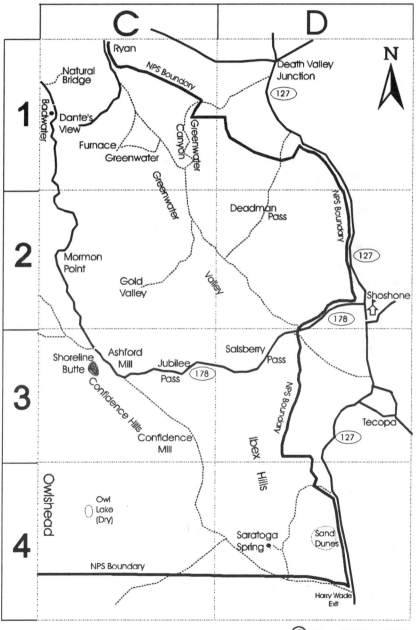

C

D

N

Ryan

Natural
Bridge

NPS Boundary

Death Valley
Junction

127

Badwater

Dante's
View

1

Furnace

Greenwater

Greenwater
Canyon

Greenwater

Deadman
Pass

NPS Boundary

127

2

Mormon
Point

Gold
Valley

Valley

127

Shoshone

178

Ashford
Mill

Salsberry
Pass

Shoreline
Butte

Confidence Hills

Jubilee
Pass

178

3

Confidence
Mill

NPS Boundary

Ibex
Hills

Tecopa

127

Owlshead

Owl
Lake
(Dry)

4

Saratoga
Spring

Sand
Dunes

NPS Boundary

Harry Wade
Exit

© Tom Willis 1995

161

To See and Do

Amargosa River (C3, C4)

This usually dry river begins north of Beatty, Nevada and runs, mostly underground, south through the Amargosa Desert east of Death Valley. At the southern end of the Black Mountains, near Saratoga Springs, the river turns north and flows into Death Valley. Some maps show this river going all the way into the salt pan near Badwater. The bed of the river contributes to the deep sand on the road from Ashford Mill to Saratoga Springs.

The origin of the word Amargosa is Spanish, and roughly translates to "bitter water of the desert." The river is home to a subspecies of pupfish, *Cyprinodon nevadensis amargosae*, these pupfish are usually found in the Death Valley portion of the river.

Anvil Spring (B3)

The name for this spring originated with the discovery of an anvil reportedly left at the spring by Asabel Bennett. The spring is located at the southern end of Butte Valley. Records indicate that miners were active in the area of this spring until the 1940s.

Ashford Mill (C3)

These mill ruins are 45.7 miles south of the Visitor Center near the junction of Badwater Road and Highway 178. The remaining mill structure is a short way off the paved road. The mill was named for the Ashford brothers, Harold, Henry, and Lewis. They owned and worked a small mine in the hills about 3 miles east of the mill from about 1907 until 1914. The brothers were able to obtain enough ore to make a modest living from their mine.

The brothers leased their mine to B. W. McCausland and his son in 1914. This pair actually built the mill to process ore and save on shipping costs. The massive foundation that still stands is due to a shipping error rather than the design of the mill. Records indicate that a double order of cement was shipped to the site and, rather than bear the cost of shipping it back, the excess was just incorporated into the construction.

The father and son team defaulted on their lease payment at the end of the first year. Mining records show that they invested $100,000 and recovered about $125,000 in ore. The Ashford's sued to regain title to their

mine and the mill in 1915. The mine was returned to the Ashfords, and they continued to work it until the 1920s.

Badwater (C1)
This pool of water is 25 miles south of the Visitor Center, at the foot of the Black Mountains. It is almost immediately below the Dante's View overlook. When at Badwater, be sure to look at the face of the cliff immediately east of the pool. Some enterprising individual, from the Park Service, has placed a sign indicating sea level.

Prior to the 1950s, Badwater was thought to be the lowest point in the United States at 279 feet below sea level. A U.S. Geological Survey team found two separate locations that measured 282 feet below sea level. For the intrepid hiker, one point is one half mile south-southwest of Natural Bridge Road and three miles north-northwest of Badwater. The other point is 4 miles north-northwest of Badwater and is almost centered between West Side Road and Badwater Road. Use the Badwater topographic map to pinpoint these locations.

There are some small desert snails *(Asiminea infirma)* and other invertebrates that live in the salt pool at Badwater. These creatures live in the saltbush and in the small seeps around the edge of the pool. Their small size makes them very hard to locate. Compounding the problem is that as you get close enough to look for them you are probably crushing them under your feet along the edge of the pool. It is best to take our word that they do actually exist and not destroy them in the process of locating them. For those of us who would like to see these small creatures continue to exist in the pool, please stay out of the water.

There is a trail that heads west out onto the salt flat from the pool at Badwater. It provides an interesting walk. As you walk along this trail, the sound of your footsteps is a lot like walking on hard packed snow. In fact, the reflection of sunlight is very much like that of fresh snow. Take your sunglasses and hat with you!

From the parking lot at Badwater you look directly west and see Telescope Peak rising 11,000 feet above the valley floor. An interesting photograph is to frame the snow capped peak's reflection in the pool.

Ballarat (A2)
This ghost town is just outside the park boundary near the southern end of Panamint Valley. The town was named for an Australian boom town of the 1800s. A post office was founded at Ballarat in June 1897. The town was the home of Seldom Seen Slim and was a major supply point for the many mines that dotted the canyons of the western Panamint Mountains.

Today there are still some adobe ruins and a few small buildings of the town remaining. This former town is well worth a visit, if you are in the area. The ruins are being protected by the resident of the town. There is a small general store, where you can obtain a refreshing cold drink, and some conversation and information about the backcountry around the town. There is also a small private campground with water. There is no telephone service in this area.

Ballarat is a jumping off point for backcountry enthusiasts who want to investigate the canyons and ghost towns of the western Panamint Mountains.

Bennett's Long Camp (B1)
This site is located on West Side Road. It is 16.2 miles south of the Visitor Center. The Bennett, Arcane, and Wade families camped here while

they waited for William Lewis Manly and John H. Rogers to return with food and a way out of the valley. Prior to this encampment the site was a Shoshone camp.

Bennett's Well (B1)
Some sources assume this well was named for Asabel Bennett of the original forty-niners. However, other sources say it may have been named for Charles "Tex" Bennett, a teamster who hauled borax out of the valley for W. T. Coleman. The story is that Tex Bennett used this site as a camp and watering spot for his mules. The well is located 23½ miles south of the Visitor Center on West Side Road.

A 1906 U.S. Geological Survey team led by E.M. Douglas, mapping water sources in the valley, reported this spring contained good water. They also determined the spring was producing up to 40 barrels of water per day at the time.

Butte Valley (B2)
This large open valley gets its name from Striped Butte, which is located near the center of this secluded valley. The valley is located at the west end of Warm Springs Canyon. A 4-wheel drive vehicle is recommended for exploring the area.

Geologist's Cabin - Butte Valley

From the north, Striped Butte is not very remarkable but the southern face leaves no mistake as to how the butte was named. The face that dominates the view is made up of a series of narrow multicolored vertical stripes. Mid-day is the best time for photographing this site.

To the west of Anvil Spring at the southern end of the valley is a small plateau. In the 1930s, a miner built a small stone cabin here. Today this is commonly called Geologist's Cabin. The plateau is sometimes referred to as "Greater View" and the view of Butte Valley from this point is magnificent.

This valley is host to a number of springs, old mines, and cabins. The most notable of these are the Greater View Spring, and Carl Mengel's mine. Most of the springs and mines are located in the southwest corner of the valley, near the base of the hills. To locate these mine sites and cabins you will need the Manly Peak topographic map.

From the plateau the road continues south and goes over Mengel Pass, through Goler Wash, and eventually brings you to Ballarat, in the Panamint Valley. At the junction at the exit to Goler Wash you want to turn north, the road to the south is closed at the China Lake Naval Weapons Center boundary.

Charcoal Kilns (B1)

These 10 beehive like structures were built in Wildrose Canyon to provide charcoal to the Modoc Mines on the western side of Panamint Valley. The Argus Mountains, home to the mines, are treeless and could not provide the fuel needed for the ore smelter. These kilns were built in the 1870s. Historical records show the kilns were designed by a Swiss engineer, built by Chinese labor, and filled with wood by Indians hired locally.

The kilns were restored by a special Navajo historic restoration team in 1971. The repairs are barely noticeable, a tribute to their craftsmanship.

The kilns are 25½ feet high and 30 to 32 feet in diameter. Each kiln has a capacity of 45 cords of wood. This would yield about 2,250 bushels of charcoal after 8 days of burning. Even though these kilns were used over 100 years ago, you can still smell faint traces of creosote, a by-product of burning wood, inside them. The conical or parabolic shape of the kilns has unusual effects on sounds, accelerating them in one area and dampening them in others.

The kilns are located 7 miles from the Wildrose Ranger Station. The second half of the ride from the ranger station is on a dirt road. Most passenger cars can drive to the kilns. It is difficult to predict the condition of the road in mid-winter, due to snow fall or rains that may wash out the road. It's best to check with the Visitor Center before beginning the 63 mile drive to the canyon. I do not recommend going beyond the kilns without a high clearance vehicle.

Confidence Mill and Hills (C3)
This mill site is located on the dirt road 6 miles south of Ashford Junction and the Highway to Jubilee Pass. The road is dirt south of the junction. This is one of the oldest gold mill sites in Death Valley. There is little, if anything, left to see here.

Of more importance is the photographer's delight called The Narrows, formed by the 500-foot high Confidence Hills. The Narrows are 7½ miles long, end to end.

Charcoal Kilns At Wildrose

Dante's View (C1)

This overlook is nothing short of breathtaking. It is only 25.6 miles from the Visitor Center. Take Highway 190 east from Furnace Creek and turn south at the Ryan/Dante's View turn-off. The road is paved the entire way. The last half mile is not suitable for vehicles towing trailers. Parking areas are provided for un-hooking and completing the drive without the additional load. When you visit Dante's View bring a jacket. The temperature can easily be 25 to 30 degrees cooler than the valley and there is always a breeze here. In the early morning it's downright cold.

The best time to visit this site is early in the day, before the heat created haze dulls the grandeur of the view. On a clear day, which is most days, you can look to the west and see both Badwater and Mt. Whitney. These are the lowest and highest points in the 48 contiguous states, less than 50 miles apart. Looking east you can see the crest of the Charleston Mountains near Las Vegas.

The best view of the valley and salt flat is found at the end of the small trail that leads to a point about a quarter mile southwest of the parking area. One story has it that this is named Poison Point, because just one drop will do it.

It's not uncommon to find amateur and sometimes professional astronomers still here in the early mornings dismantling their gear. If you're into star gazing, I do not know of another easily accessible, treeless, smogless, lightless place that has a seemingly endless eastern horizon, and that is on public land. Be sure to get permission from the Park Service before attempting to spend the night in the parking area.

Dayton-Harris Grave (B1)
This gravesite is on West Side Road, a short way from Shorty's Well. A stone monument has been erected at the site to pay tribute to these two men that contributed to the history of the valley.

This is the final resting place of Jim Dayton a teamster on the 20-Mule Team wagons and later the manager of Greenland Ranch (now Furnace Creek Ranch). Dayton died on his way to get supplies in August 1899.

He was found dead at this site by searchers who went looking for him when he did not return from his trip. His dog was found alive, still guarding his master; but the horses, still hitched to the wagon, had died of thirst.

Frank "Shorty" Harris, a long time friend of Dayton's, was one of the prospectors credited with the discovery of the Bullfrog Mine at Rhyolite. Harris died in 1934 and his final wish was to be buried beside Jim Dayton in the valley they loved. He also wanted his epitaph to be "Here lies Shorty Harris, a single blanket jackass prospector."

Eagle Borax Works (B1)
This site is a little over 20 miles from the Visitor Center on West Side Road. The history behind this site is discussed in Chapter 1 as part of the borax history of the valley. Little remains of this short-lived borax works. Isadore Daunet staked claim to this site after Aaron Winters discovered borax at Cottonball Marsh. The output here was so poor in quality that it could not sustain the operation.

At one point there was a small forest of Tamarisk trees here. However, they are not natural to the area and were literally emptying the nearby ponds of water. These ponds support migratory waterfowl and local wildlife, so the Tamarisk trees had to go.

Stone Building At Furnace

Furnace (C1)
In the heart of the Greenwater Valley are the remnants of yet another boomtown. When I was last there the site consisted on the typical ghost town, tin can dumps and a single small stone building nestled at the foot of a small hill. This was one of a couple of towns that blossomed here as the result of a highly overrated copper discovery in 1905. The copper deposits were not as large or concentrated as they were originally thought to be. This coupled with the financial panic of 1907, spelled the end for the town.

Galena Canyon (B2)
This canyon is off West Side Road, 14½ miles south of Bennett's Long Camp. You need 4-wheel drive to explore this area. A short hike beyond the end of the road brings you to several old talc mines. Some sources say that the talc mines in this canyon were being worked into the 1980s.

Gold Valley (C2)
As you drive the dirt road through Greenwater Valley, be sure and visit this area in the southwestern section of the Greenwater area. Gold Valley was named by hopeful prospectors from Greenwater. They were so confident that they named the valley before any ore was found. Very little, if

any, was ever found. When their hopes did not pay off they left the valley but the name remained. At the end of the road you can hike a half mile down to Willow Spring and Willow Creek. If you want to hike in from Death Valley, Gold Valley and Willow Spring are just east of Mormon Point.

Goler Wash (A3)
This is actually a canyon and wash that descends the west side of the Panamint Mountains. It provides a 4-wheel drive route from Mengel Pass to Panamint Valley. Goler Wash is named for John Goler, a forty-niner with the Jayhawker Party and a desert prospector. Goler returned to the valley to look for gold after the Jayhawkers reached their destination in California.

Gravel Well (B2)
This spring is 5½ miles south of Bennett's Well on West Side Road The spring is on the west side of the road. It was one of the rest stops on the 20-Mule Team route. The water at this spring has been reported as sweet, but is does have traces of salt in it.

Greenwater (C1)
This is another mining boom town in Greenwater Valley. It too was doomed when the copper and the money ran out in 1907. Greenwater was the center of activity during the copper boom. This town had a newspaper of sorts, the "Chuckwalla." The old press used to print this paper can be seen behind the Borax Museum at Furnace Creek.

As you survey the site of Greenwater, it is hard to imagine that several thousand people settled here within the first month of the town's founding. Besides a newspaper, the town had a bank, post office, drugstore, and telephone service. All this, and no water, it had to be brought in by wagon. The town was short lived. The newspaper was first published in January 1907 and 10 months later it and the town were history.

Greenwater Canyon (C1)
This small, somewhat narrow canyon is home to some of the best examples of Petroglyphs to be found anywhere in the valley. Most maps show a road passing through this canyon and connecting with Highway 127 near Death Valley Junction. This road is now closed and vehicles are not permitted within this canyon.

The canyon is located about 15½ miles from the Dante's View turnoff on Highway 190. A high clearance vehicle is required to drive to the mouth of the canyon. After parking at the mouth of the canyon, hike in a short way, walking in the middle of the canyon surveying the rock faces on both sides. You will soon see many Petroglyphs all over the rocks. Most of the drawings seem to be found on the upper two thirds of the canyon walls. You can carefully climb over the lower rocks to get a close up look at the drawings. Be very careful when climbing not to dislodge loose rocks. If you are not sure of your footing do not risk a fall, help is a long way off. Also remember these rocks are significant historical artifacts and are not to be disturbed, moved, or damaged.

Since the Petroglyphs are on rocks on both sides of the canyon, you can take pictures most times of the day. Most of the rocks have a heavy coating of Desert Varnish. Because of this you may have to wait for the right angle of the sun to take a picture.

Greenwater Valley (C1,C2,D2)
This long narrow valley is on the eastern side of the Black Mountains. The valley got its name from the little water found in the area. It had a faint green tinge to it. Throughout this valley very little indication remains of the mining and prospecting activity that took place here.

172

Access to the area is via a dirt road heading south off the paved road to Dante's View. This road connects with Highway 178 at Jubilee Pass 30 miles to the south. Generally the road is passable with a high clearance vehicle but, at times, you may find some deep sand crossings in some washes. Always investigate any sand before attempting to cross it if you do not have 4-wheel drive.

Hanapauh Canyon (B1)
This canyon is off West Side Road. The turn off for this canyon is just to the west of Shorty's Well. The drive up the canyon requires 4-wheel drive. The end of the road is near Hanapauh Spring, on the eastern face of the Panamint Mountains just below Telescope Peak.

Harry Wade Exit (D4)
This site is at the southeastern most point of the park. It is at the junction of the dirt road from Saratoga Springs at Highway 127 about 30 miles north of Baker. This is presumed to be where Harry Wade and his family left the valley. Wade was the only member of the original forty-niners to get a wagon out intact. All the other parties either abandoned, damaged, or burned their wagons before leaving.

Johnson Canyon (B2)
The road into Johnson Canyon is 4½ miles south of Bennett's Well on West Side Road. The canyon goes up into the eastern side of the Panamint Mountains. The 10 mile ride requires 4-wheel drive. At the end of the road is a small spring and a trail that goes about another mile to the site of Hungry Bill's Ranch. The last time I was there, I found some stone walls, a corral, and the remnants of a cabin.

Hungry Bill was the brother of Panamint Tom, a Shoshone Chief. He was deeded the land at the top of this canyon for his services as an army scout during the Modoc Wars. Hungry Bill is reputed to have sold some of the food he raised to the miners at Panamint City. There is a trail that connects his ranch site with the site of the former town.

Jubilee Pass (C3)
This is the first pass you encounter if you are driving east on Highway 178 from Ashford Mill. The pass is 53.9 miles south of the Visitor Center. The elevation of the pass is 1290 feet. This route takes you to the town of Shoshone.

Mengel Pass (B3)
This pass is at the crest of the Panamint Mountains between Butte Valley
and Goler Wash. It was named for Carl Mengel, a miner who worked
claims in this area for years. There is a small brass plaque on a marker at
the pass dedicated to Mengel. Various stories report that his grave is actually under the marker at the pass.

Mengel's mine and his home were located near Greater View Spring and
Russell Camp. Mengel's home was reported to have 18 inch thick walls
that insulated it from both heat and cold.

Mormon Point (C2)
This point is on Badwater Road, 34.7 miles south of the Visitor Center. It
is named in honor of the Mormon miners who worked mines in the area.
Hiking east from the road at Mormon Point brings you into Gold Valley
by way of Willow Creek and Willow Spring.

Natural Bridge Canyon (C1)
This is a walk-in canyon in the Black Mountains, 17½ miles south of the
Visitor Center. A 1½ mile dirt road leads up to the beginning of the trail.
The canyon with its sheer walls, is spanned by a massive "bridge." This
was left behind as the canyon was eroded by run-off from the mountains.

The "bridge" can be seen at the end of an easy ¾ mile walk from the parking area.

Owlshead Mountains (B4,C4)
This small horseshoe shaped chain of mountains is at the southern end of the Panamint Range. These mountains are home to two dry lakes, Lost Lake and Owl Lake, and a number of old mining ventures. There are no open roads into this area.

There is an interesting old Epsom Salts mine and works on the northwest side of the mountains near Wingate Wash and the China Lake NWC boundary (closed to public). The salts were discovered in 1917. In 1919 Thomas Wright bought the rights to the claim. He had a great plan for transporting the salts from the mine on a mono-rail. This single steel rail was supported on a wooden A-frame structure about 3 feet high.

This mono-rail went 28 miles from the mine site, Crystal Camp, to the Trona Railroad at Searles Lake. Wright spent every dollar of his company's money in trying to make his mono-rail idea work. He was plagued by under-powered engines and continual breakdowns. When he finally had an engine powerful enough for his needs, the wooden A-frame wouldn't take the weight and collapsed. He did ship some salts from his mine, but they were mixed with so much desert dust the ore's value could not pay for the mining effort. The mono-rail is inside China Lake NWC.

Panamint City (A2)
This silver mining town was in Surprise Canyon in the Panamint Mountains at an elevation of 6,500 feet. Silver was discovered here in 1872 by Richard Jacobs, William Kennedy, and Robert Stewart. They named their find the "Wonder of the World." The initial reports and assays indicated this discovery would rival the Comstock Lode of Virginia City, Nevada.

By the fall of 1873 a hundred claims had been staked in the small valley at the top of Surprise Canyon. At the time there were about 20 people living in the camp. In the winter of 1874 Panamint City was the biggest town in the area with a population of about 2,000 people and more than 600 mine claims.

In addition to more than 20 saloons, Panamint City had two banks, three doctors, a couple of general goods stores, and Death Valley's first newspaper. During the first half of 1875 the Surprise Valley Mill and Water Company built a reservoir, a 20 stamp mill, and a smelter furnace. This furnace and chimney is reported to have required over a half million bricks and cost more than $200,000 to build.

During the town's heyday, silver shipments were a dangerous undertaking due to the distance between Panamint City and towns with rail connections. It is said that even Wells Fargo was reluctant to carry silver out of the town. A solution was found, the silver was cast into large balls weighing about 450 pounds. With this novel approach not one shipment was lost to thieves.

Panamint City and the Wonder of the World were not destined to rival the Comstock Lode. A bank panic in 1875 took the excitement and money out of mining stocks. Then in the summer of 1876 a flash flood washed most of what remained of the town out of the small valley. After this some efforts were made to mine the area but none were really successful.

Today, you can visit this historic town by driving up Surprise Canyon from Ballarat. As of this writing the road to the town had not been closed by the Wilderness Act. Be sure to confirm the status of the road with the Park Service. This trip will require a team of 4-wheel drive vehicles equipped with winches and skilled drivers. About 3 miles up the canyon you will find Chris Wicht Camp, beyond this the road will become more rugged. The town is about 6 miles from the camp. Surprise Canyon is not a drive through canyon, you will have to come back down this road to exit.

Most visitors may find it easier to simply hike the canyon from Chris Wicht Camp. This will provide a good work-out. There is a trail from Panamint City to Hungry Bill's Ranch at the top of Johnson Canyon. This hike will take you over the crest of the Panamint Mountains through Panamint Pass. This trip is best undertaken by hikers prepared to camp overnight on the trail.

Pleasant Canyon (A2)
This canyon is immediately east of the Ballarat ghost town. Four wheel drive is required to travel by vehicle in this canyon. The entrance to the canyon is just outside the boundary of the park. Clair Camp is located in this canyon. This camp is also the approximate location of the park

boundary. To be safe verify the status of the road beyond the camp with the Park Service before undertaking a trip into the canyon.

The site of the World Beater Mine is located near the top of this canyon, inside the park boundary. This gold mine was discovered in 1896. This mine was the purpose for the founding of Ballarat. The Montgomery brothers, Bob and George were the founders of the mine. Bob Montgomery was the investor that developed the town of Skidoo in the 1920s.

Ryan (C1)

This mining camp still exists on private property near the junction of Highway 190 and Dante's View Road. The property belongs to the U.S. Borax and Chemical Corporation. Although you can see some of the buildings for the road, the area is closed to visitors.

In the 1920s and 1930s Ryan was the site of the Valley View Hotel operated by the Pacific Coast Borax Company. The Death Valley Railroad ran from Death Valley Junction to Ryan and on to the Lila C borax mine. The borax company, in conjunction with Union Pacific Railroad, would bring guests to the valley to see the wonders offered by the desert. A locomotive from the Death Valley Railroad is on exhibit behind the Borax Museum at Furnace Creek Ranch.

Salsberry Pass (D3)

This is the second pass you encounter when driving east on Highway 178 from Ashford Mill. The elevation is 3310 feet. The pass was named for Jack Salsberry, know by some as Death Valley's most persistent mine promoter. Salsberry was responsible for the completion of the road over this pass to ship lead ore out of the valley during World War One.

Salt Wells (B2)

Located on West Side Road near the road to Galena Canyon, this well has been reported as dry in one source and having sweet water in another. The last time I was in the area I did not find any water, but that visit was during the last major drought of the 1990's in California.

Saratoga Springs (D4)

This spring and ponds are in the extreme southern part of the park. They constitute the largest natural body of water in the Mojave Desert. This area can be reached only by a dirt road. The easiest approach is from

Saratoga Springs

Highway 127 at Harry Wade Exit. The 28 mile long road, south from Ashford Mill, usually requires 4-wheel drive due to the deep sand found in the bed of the Amargosa River.

In years past there was a large grove of Tamarisk trees here, but they were removed because they were threatening the existence of the ponds. The spring is home to its own species of pupfish, *Cyprinodon nevadensis nevadensis*. The ponds are also a stop over for migratory waterfowl.

Evidence has been found here indicating a prehistoric people, the Saratoga Spa people, once lived here.

From Highway 127, take Saratoga Springs Road (dirt) west for about 6 miles. The route you want turns north at this point, continuing west eventually takes you to Ashford Junction. The road takes you about 3 miles north to the base of the Ibex Hills. The small dunes you see to the east are the Ibex Dunes. When you get near the hills follow the road to the west along the foot of the hills to the spring and pond.

Shoreline Butte (C3)
This small hill is to the west of Badwater Road just west of Ashford Mill. The hill is only 650 feet high. The significance of this hill is that it is

Telescope Peak From Eagle Borax Works

marked with small terraces cut by the receding waters of Lake Manly. About one million years ago, this lake filled the valley to an estimated depth of 600 feet. As of this writing there is no sign on the road to indicate this site.

Telescope Peak (B1)
This is the highest mountain in the Park. It dominates the western horizon from all points in southern Death Valley. The summit of the mountain is 11,049 feet above sea level.

The peak can be reached by taking an 8 mile hike that starts at Mahogany Flat Campground, at the top of Wildrose Canyon. John Thorndyke, a miner, once dreamed of building a hotel atop the mountain. He was never able to do this, but did succeed in building some small cabins at what is now Thorndike Campground.

Warm Springs Canyon (B2)
This drive-through canyon can be reached with a high clearance vehicle from West Side Road This canyon was also one of the winter camps for the Indians of the Death Valley area. The road through the canyon provides the easiest access to Butte Valley. The turnoff for this road is 3 miles west of the junction with Badwater Road.

This canyon was the site of extensive talc mining until the late 1980s. The land has since been donated to the Park Service and is in the process of being made environmentally stable.

West Side Road (B1,B2,C2,C3)
This well graded dirt road is a north-south route on the western side of Death Valley. It follows the fans along the base of the Panamint Mountains west of the salt flats. The north end of the road cuts across Devil's Golf Course.

At times the road gets "wash board" bumpy but most vehicles should be able to travel over it if driven carefully. It does provide access to many sites that are associated with much of the history of the area. A drive down this road is well worth your time.

Wildrose Canyon (A1,B1)
This canyon is located in the Panamint Mountains, west of Telescope Peak. There is a paved road through the first seven miles of the canyon. The road is dirt the remainder of the way to the Charcoal Kilns and the campgrounds beyond. There are no services other than a small campground and a ranger station located in the canyon.

This canyon earned its name when early explorers found wild roses growing in the area. In the past this area was home to a large burro population. Today, through effective wildlife management efforts, you will rarely see a burro in this area. The burros were removed from the area because of the negative impact they were having on both plant and animal life.

The major attraction of the area is the Charcoal Kilns. There are also two campgrounds at the end of the canyon. Mahogany Flat Campground was named for the Desert Mahogany trees found in the area. Thorndike Campground was named for John Thorndyke, a miner. He did finally build a few tourist cabins at Mahogany Flat, but these are gone today.

If you are driving a motorhome or towing a trailer, Wildrose Canyon may not be advisable for you. The road is limited to vehicles less than 24 feet in total length, there are some very tight turns as you approach the mouth of the canyon. The road beyond Wildrose Canyon to Ballarat and Trona is graded but not paved. It may be very rough due to recent storm activity in the area. I recommend you verify the status of this road with the Park Service before planning a trip through Wildrose to Ballarat and beyond.

Wingate Wash (B3)
This large wash is southwest of Ashford Mill ruins. It is the southern part of the borax wagon route out of the Valley. The wagons from both Eagle Borax Works and Harmony Borax Works used this route on their way to either Mojave or Daggett.

This wash and Long Valley provide a physical separation for the southern Panamint Mountains and the Owlshead Mountains. This natural route out of the valley gently climbs from the valley floor to an elevation of about 2000 feet without any significantly steep areas.

Today, you can only explore about the first ten miles of the wash. The remainder is part of the China Lake Naval Weapons Center and sadly you are not welcome there. If you are determined to investigate this area, you can write to the Commanding Officer at the base and ask for written permission to enter the base. The Navy takes any unauthorized intrusion into their land very seriously.

In addition to the role this area played in the borax mining era of the valley it is also home to Crystal Camp. This was the site of an Epsom Salt mine and a unique mono-rail. (See Owlshead Mountains)

Appendix A
Services Outside the Park

Area Motels

Area Code 619
Changed To 760

Amargosa Valley, NV 89020

Desert Village Motel		(702) 372-1405

Baker, CA 92309

Bun Boy Motel	72155 Baker Blvd.	(619) 733-4363
Royal Hawaiian Motel	200 W. Baker Blvd.	(619) 733-4326
Wills Fargo Motel	72252 Baker Blvd.	(619) 733-4477

Beatty, NV 89003

Burro Inn	P.O. Box 3	(702) 553-2225
El Portal Motel	P.O. Box 336	(702) 553-2912
Exchange Club	P.O. Box 97	(702) 553-2333
Phoenix Inn	P.O. Box 503	(800) 845-7401
Stagecoach	P.O. Box 836	(800) 424-4946

Big Pine, CA 93513

Big Pine Motel	370 S. Main	(619) 938-2282
Big Pine Resort Cottages	505 S. Main	(619) 938-2922
Glacier Lodge	P.O. Box 327	(619) 872-9271
Starlight Motel	511 S. Main	(619) 938-2011

Bishop, CA 93514

Best Western	1025 N. Main St.	(619) 873-3543
Bishop Rodeway Inn	150 E. Elm St.	(619) 873-3564
Bishop Inn	805 N. Main St.	(800) 576-4080
Elms Hotel	233 E. Elm St.	(619) 873-8118
El Rancho Motel	274 Lagoon St.	(619) 872-9251
Lakeview Motel	2296 Sierra Hi-way	(619) 873-4019
Mountain View Motel	730 West Line St.	(619) 873-4242
National 9	1005 N. Main St.	(619) 873-8426
Outdoorsman Motor Lodge	651 N. Main St.	(619) 873-6381
Piute Lodge	796 West Line St.	(619) 873-6391
Sportsman's Motel	636 N. Main St.	(619) 872-2423

Bishop, CA 93514 (cont'd)

Starlite Motel	192 Short St.	(619) 873-4912
Thunderbird Inn	190 W. Pine St.	(619) 873-4215
Townhouse Motel	625 N. Main St.	(619) 872-4541

Death Valley, CA 92328

Furnace Creek Ranch	P.O. Box 1	(619) 786-2345
Furnace Creek Inn	P.O. Box 1	(619) 786-2361
Stovepipe Wells Village		(619) 786-2387

Death Valley Junction, CA 92328

Amargosa Hotel		(619) 852-4441

Independence, CA 93526

Ray's Den Motel	405 N. Edwards	(619) 878-2122
Winnedumah Country Inn	P.O. Box 24	(619) 878-2040

Las Vegas, NV

Las Vegas Room Finders		(800) 234-8342
A-Z Reservation Service		(800) 634-6915
Las Vegas Referrals		(800) 999-9144

Lone Pine, CA 93545

Alabama Hills Inn	1920 S. Main	(619) 876-8700
Dow Villa Motel	310 S. Main	(619) 876-5521
Best Western Frontier	1008 S. Main	(619) 876-5571
Mt. Whitney Motel	305 N. Main	(619) 876-4207
National 9 Motel	633 S. Main	(619) 876-5555
Portal Motel	425 S. Main	(619) 876-5930

Olancha, CA 93549

Ranch Motel	Hi-way 395	(619) 764-2387
Rustic Motel	P.O. Box 173	(619) 764-2209

Panamint Springs, CA 93522

Panamint Springs Resort	P.O. Box 395	(619) 764-2010
	Ridgecrest, CA 93556	

Ridgecrest, CA 93555

BevLen Haus B&B	809 N. Sanders	(619) 375-1988
Carriage Inn	901 N. China Lake Blvd.	(619) 446-7910
Econolodge	201 Inyokern Rd.	(619) 446-2551
El Ranchito Motel	1445 Inyokern Rd.	(619) 446-6209
El Rancho Motel	507 S. China Lake Blvd.	(619) 375-9731
Heritage Suites	919 N. Heritage Dr.	(619) 446-7951
Heritage Inn	1050 N. Norma	(619) 446-6543
Motel 6	535 S. China Lake Blvd.	(619) 375-6866
Pioneer Motel	416 S. China Lake Blvd.	(619) 375-1591
Ridgecrest Motel	401 S. China Lake Blvd.	(619) 375-8406

Shoshone, CA 92384

Shoshone Motel	P.O. Box 67	(619) 852-4335

Tecopa Hot Springs, CA 92384

Delight's Hot Spa	P.O. Box 36	(619) 852-4343
Hot Springs Resort	P.O. Box 420	(619) 852-4373

Bus Service

Greyhound	Lone Pine, CA	(619) 876-5300
Greyhound	Ridgecrest, CA	(619) 371-1302

Emergencies
Dial 911 0r (619)-786-2330

Highway Information

California	(800) 427-7623
Nevada	(702) 793-1313

R.V. Parks
Beatty, NV 89003

Burro Inn RV Park	Hiway 95 & 3rd St.	(702) 553-2445
Kay's Korral RV Park	Hiway 95 N	(702) 553-2732
Rio Rancho RV Park	E Hiway 95 N	(702) 553-2238
Space Station RV Park	Hiway 95	(702) 553-9039

Pahrump, NV 89041

Pahrump Station RV Park	E. Loop Road	(702) 727-5100
Rosemary's RV Park	S. Bridge	(702) 727-4488
Seven Palms RV Park	Hiway 372 & Linda	(702) 727-6091

Ridgecrest, CA 93555

Ridgecrest Blvd RV Park	W Ridgecrest Blvd.	(619) 375-5843

Trona, CA 93562

Trona RV Park	Trona Rd	(619) 372-5371

Sheriff's Dept. (Inyo County)

Death Valley Sub-station	Furnace Creek	(619) 786-2238

TDD (California Relay Service)
{Public Service - Voice to TDD Link}

Voice	(800) 735-2922
TDD	(800) 735-2929

Towing

AAA (Automobile Club of Southern California)	(800) 400-4222
Furnace Creek Garage	(619) 786-2232
National Automobile Club	(800) 622-2130

Appendix B

Miles Between Selected Sites

(Totals Rounded to Nearest Whole Mile)

Copyright © 1995 Tom Willis

To (Column) / **From (Row)**

From (Row)	Aguereberry Point	Artist's Palette	Ashford Mill	Badwater	Butte Valley	Charcoal Kilns	Dante's View	Devil's Cornfield	Devil's Golfcourse	Eureka Dunes	Golden Canyon	Harmony Borax Works	Hells Gate	Keane Wonder Mine	Natural Bridge	Panamint Springs Resort	Rhyolite	Salt Creek	Salt Works and Tram	Sand Dunes Day Area	Saratoga Spring	Scotty's Castle	Stovepipe Wells Village	Titus Canyon (Start)	Ubehebe Crater	Visitor Center
Artist's Palette	67																									
Ashford Mill	98	43																								
Badwater	72	16	27																							
Butte Valley	121	65	26	49																						
Charcoal Kilns	22	99	142	115	143																					
Dante's View	78	33	68	41	90	100																				
Devil's Cornfield	34	32	55	28	77	46	44																			
Devil's Golfcourse	66	12	34	7	56	82	34	35																		
Eureka Dunes	115	110	141	115	158	122	121	116	109																	
Golden Canyon	57	10	42	16	59	67	26	25	10	99																
Harmony Borax Works	80	16	47	21	64	60	27	20	15	94	5															
Hells Gate	43	62	93	67	110	73	61	73	34	86	51	46														
Keane Wonder Mine	50	35	66	40	83	46	34	81	16	93	24	19	7													
Natural Bridge	68	10	32	5	54	76	39	36	5	110	13	16	62	35												
Panamint Springs Resort	39	69	110	74	117	34	80	64	34	115	58	52	45	53	69											
Rhyolite	61	53	84	58	101	117	27	52	37	101	42	22	15	53	53	63										
Salt Creek	39	59	33	76	48	101	70	64	39	85	27	28	14	22	53	63	41									
Salt Works and Tram	92	122	153	127	170	89	121	133	45	122	105	98	53	116	122	105	53	94								
Sand Dunes Day Area	36	34	65	39	82	2	33	45	18	47	17	10	38	47	38	34	47	8	91							
Saratoga Spring	125	57	26	52	52	93	59	98	79	167	78	68	119	92	126	57	110	179	92	92						
Scotty's Castle	71	68	99	73	116	40	67	50	81	50	56	68	92	60	74	69	60	40	127	35	125					
Stovepipe Wells Village	28	39	70	44	87	6	38	50	37	85	28	23	52	33	30	40	58	3	44	8	96	44				
Titus Canyon (Start)	55	75	106	80	123	21	86	73	74	99	59	64	59	20	60	44	111	58	129	38	132	23	27			
Ubehebe Crater	74	70	101	75	118	26	96	83	69	40	54	59	54	15	46	60	107	13	127	72	53	33	46	58		
Visitor Center	53	15	46	20	63	21	40	61	14	95	4	4	20	38	54	15	20	18	38	15	20	73	33	24	55	
Zabriskie Point	58	16	47	21	66	26	21	66	6	100	6	52	17	59	17	59	43	18	112	25	73	58	29	38	60	5

To determine the distance between two points, first select the row name for your starting point.

Then select the column name that corresponds to your desired destination.

The approximate distance is the number where the column and row intersect.

187

Kilometers Between Selected Sites

(Totals Rounded to Nearest Whole Km)

Copyright © 1995 Tom Willis

From (Row) \ To (Column)	Aguereberry Point	Artist's Pallette	Ashford Mill	Badwater	Butte Valley	Charcoal Kilns	Dante's View	Devil's Cornfield	Devil's Golfcourse	Eureka Dunes	Golden Canyon	Harmony Borax Works	Hells Gate	Keane Wonder Mine	Natural Bridge	Panamint Springs Resort	Rhyolite	Salt Creek	Salt Works and Tram	Sand Dunes Day Area	Saratoga Spring	Scotty's Castle	Stovepipe Wells Village	Titus Canyon (Start)	Ubehebe Crater	Visitor Center
Artist's Palette	108																									
Ashford Mill	158	69																								
Badwater	116	26	43																							
Butte Valley	195	105	42	79																						
Charcoal Kilns	35	159	228	185	230																					
Dante's View	126	53	109	66	145	161																				
Devil's Cornfield	55	51	88	45	124	74	71																			
Devil's Golfcourse	106	19	55	11	90	132	71	56																		
Eureka Dunes	185	177	227	185	254	196	195	187	175																	
Golden Canyon	92	16	68	26	95	108	42	40	16	159																
Harmony Borax Works	129	26	76	34	103	97	43	32	24	151	8															
Hells Gate	69	100	150	108	177	97	117	13	98	138	82	74														
Keane Wonder Mine	80	56	106	64	134	130	74	26	55	150	39	31	11													
Natural Bridge	109	16	51	8	87	122	63	58	8	177	21	26	100	56												
Panamint Springs Resort	63	111	177	119	188	55	129	58	109	185	93	85	72	84	111											
Rhyolite	98	85	135	93	163	113	103	43	84	163	68	60	24	35	85	101										
Salt Creek	63	45	53	122	77	63	8	43	8	137	27	19	23	19	45	66	35									
Salt Works and Tram	148	196	246	214	274	140	214	195	143	179	171	158	169	196	85	187	151	187								
Sand Dunes Day Area	58	55	105	63	132	72	72	3	53	126	37	29	16	27	55	61	13	146	13							
Saratoga Spring	201	92	42	84	214	158	150	95	269	117	191	148	92	203	137	177	288	148	146	201						
Scotty's Castle	114	109	159	117	187	130	127	64	108	80	68	80	111	119	97	64	204	56	201	148	56					
Stovepipe Wells Village	45	63	113	71	140	60	80	10	61	137	45	37	24	35	53	48	64	53	18	134	13	154				
Titus Canyon (Start)	88	121	171	129	198	117	138	34	119	159	95	103	32	21	64	93	121	5	43	179	37	212	88			
Ubehebe Crater	119	113	163	121	190	134	154	64	111	64	87	95	72	84	113	74	208	97	71	204	61	179	13	74		
Visitor Center	85	24	74	32	101	98	42	34	23	153	6	32	76	32	64	87	61	21	172	116	32	56	39	53	88	
Zabriskie Point	93	26	76	34	103	106	34	42	24	161	6	10	84	40	27	95	69	29	180	117	47	61	93	40	97	8

To determine the distance between two points, first select the row name for your starting point.
Then select the column name that corresponds to your desired destination.
The approximate distance is the number where the column and row intersect.

Bibliography

Adkison, Ron; *A Hiker's Guide to California*; Falcon Press Publishing Co, Helena, Mt; 1987

Clark, Lew and Ginny; *High Mountains & Deep Valleys*; Western Trails Publications, San Luis Obispo, Ca; 1978

Decker, Barbara and Robert; *Road Guide to Death Valley*; Double Decker Press, Mariposa, Ca; 1989

Federal Writers Project; *Death Valley; the 1938 WPA guide*; Olympus Press, Santa Barbara, Ca, 1991

Foster, Lynne; *Adventuring in the California Desert*; Sierra Club Books, San Francisco, Ca; 1987

Gebhardt, Chuck; *Backpacking Death Valley*; Chuck Gebhardt, San Jose, Ca, 1985

Greene, Linda, and Latschar, John; *Historic Resource Study, a history of mining in Death Valley National Monument*; National Park Service, Denver, Co; 1981

Gudde, Erwin G; *California Place Names*; University of California, Berkeley, Ca; 1969

Historical Preservation Committee of the Timbisha Shoshone Tribe; *The Timbisha Shoshone Tribe and their Living Valley*; Chalfant Press, Bishop, Ca; 1994

Hunt, Charles; *Death Valley: Geology, Ecology, Archaeology*; University of California Press, Los Angeles, Ca; 1975

Kirk, Ruth; *Exploring Death Valley*; Stanford University Press, Stanford, Ca 1981

Kyle, Douglas; *Historic Spots in California*; Stanford University Press, Stanford Ca, 1990

Lingenfelter, Richard E; *Death Valley and The Amargosa*; University of California Press, Los Angeles, Ca; 1986

Manly, William Lewis; *Death Valley in '49*; University Microfilms Inc, Ann Arbor, Mi; 1966

McCracken, Robert D; *A History of Beatty, Nevada*; Nye County Press, Tonopah, Nv; 1992

McKinley, W. L; *Native Fishes of Arid Lands: a dwindling resource of the desert southwest*; U.S. Dept. of Agriculture, Fort Collins, Co; 1991

McMahon, James A; *Deserts*; Alfred A. Knopf, Inc, New York, NY; 1985

Miller, Ronald D; *Mines of the High Desert*; La Siesta Press, Glendale, Ca; 1992

Mitchell, Roger, *Death Valley Jeep Trails*, La Siesta Press, Glendale, Ca; 1975

Mitchell, Roger; *Inyo Mono Jeep Trails*; La Siesta Press, Glendale, Ca; 1969

National Park Foundation; *The Complete Guide To America's National Parks*; National Park Foundation, Washington, D. C.; 1991

Palmer, T. S; *Place Names of the Death Valley Region*; Sagebrush Press, Morongo Valley, Ca; 1980

Raven, Peter H; *Native Shrubs of Southern California*; University of California Press, Berkeley, Ca; 1966

Schoenherr, Allan A; *A Natural History of California*; University of California Press, Berkeley, Ca: 1995

Union Pacific Railroad; *Death Valley - Region of Mystery, Desolation, and Grandeur*; Rand - McNally and Co, Chicago; 1927

Index